WILLING
TO CHANGE

WILLING TO CHANGE

Second Edition

AUTOBIOGRAPHY:
GEORGE MARRERO

XULON PRESS

Xulon Press
2301 Lucien Way #415
Maitland, FL 32751
407.339.4217
www.xulonpress.com

Printed in the United States of America.

ISBN-13: 978-1-5456-4055-5

TABLE OF CONTENTS

INTRODUCTION

AN EXPERIENCE THAT ALWAYS SURPRISED ME as an adolescent was to be treated good by a police officer. To me it was surprising; weren't they the enemies? I mean this is what we were taught growing up. That cops hate us for being minorities. Yet, on one or two occasions when my friends and I were stopped by cops for petty stuff. Like sneaking into the train station instead of paying and the police were called. They would intervene with us. Even take us into their police station, in the train station. But I can clearly remember the cops being nice, and even giving us words of advice like "stay in school," or "stay out of trouble." One officer even zipped up my jacket, then pat me on my shoulder. "What was going on?" I thought to myself.

On another occasion while jogging on the streets towards the track field, a police officer that was walking my way made eye contact with me. I stared hard; I was not afraid of the enemy. He, smiled and said "good morning." It was confusing, why were they nice? I truly believed cops were unemotional, nonhuman, lacking empathy, mechanical beings, and they were out to get us. Yet, the truth is, I was never arrested until I started committing crimes.

Chapter 1

MY CHILDHOOD IN WILLIS AVENUE

"HEY, NOW THAT THE FAMILY IS ALL TOGETHER let's take a walk around the block!" Yelled the older boys. "We are coming too," join in the smaller kids. It was a nice sunny, summer day that had us excited. Our group of about six boys, was made up of siblings and cousins. Ranging from ages five to eleven. We walked around our neighborhood block sharing stories and looking into the storefronts. We stopped by a pet shop to look at the puppies. Suddenly, a bigger group of kids, and clearly older than we were stopped us. "Is this your click, what's the name of your gang?" Fear flushed my chest, I froze. "I hope Danny isn't dumb enough to say we're a gang." I thought to myself. "No, no, we're just family taking a walk around the block." Answered my older brother Danny. I guessed he was just as scared as I was. Danny was my older brother from the same mother, but a different father.

"Go on by then," said the boy that had stopped us. His whole click moved aside and let us continue our walk. It didn't take much to know the kid talking was the leader of his gang. As a kid it seemed to me as if there were gangs everywhere in this neighborhood.

There were a lot of abandoned buildings in this neighborhood. Many of the gangs claim these empty buildings or empty lots as their turfs. But as kids we would go and play in these buildings. One day, my siblings and I were playing in the back yard of one of these empty building. Smash! A large pair of steel scissors crashed right into the wall, between where my sister and I stood. "Run!" Evelyn yelled out. As we started running, we looked up towards the fire escape where the scissors came from. Two guys were running down the fire escape to get to us. We knew they were gang members because of the clothe they wore. We were so afraid, and ran out of there as quick as we could. We knew gang members had thrown kids off the roof on prior occasions for being on their turf.

Willis Avenue was a predominant Puerto Rican neighborhood. There was even a theater named *'Teatro Puerto Rico.'* One block behind the blocked we lived on. Here the people were tough and violent. I can remember seeing a knife fight between two women. They were slashing at each other's arms and faces. While the people just formed a human circle around them. The human circle had more than one purpose, it did not let anyone step in and stop the fight, but it also did not allow the people fighting to coward up and run away. You had to fight until someone really lost or the police came.

Getting out of school one afternoon at about 3:00 p.m. everyone was running across the street where a crowd was already formed. "Hit him, hit him!" "That punk!" "Bust him up!" I couldn't see who was fighting because again the human circle was formed. I was approximately six years of age and not very tall. "Who is it, who is fighting?" No one answered me. The fight had everyone's attention. All of a sudden, I was able to see one of the boys fighting. It was my best friend's older brother. The truth is he wasn't even fighting, he was getting beat up badly. His mouth was full of blood and he was screaming. From my perception he was trying to run, but the adults were not letting him run. He put his arms on top of a car, yelling, but the boy pulled him back into the circle and beat him some more as the people cheered the beating on. I could hear adults warning others, "No one better stop the fight or call the cops."

I felt lost and confused, this was my friend's brother and I couldn't do nothing and no one else cared to do anything. I wondered who he had disrespect to cause him to get beat up this bad, and at the same time have the adult's approval for the beating. I don't remember ever seeing my friend Roy again after this terrible beating his brother received that day. This is the way the neighborhood ran, people had to play by the street rules.

On another occasion as my family and I walked down one of the streets of this pandora's box of a neighborhood. We saw a crowd of people, something like the human circle. Though, this time there was less people and they were looking down to the grown. We looked and saw a young man, laying on the floor. He was almost unconscious, and appeared to be moaning a bit. Next to him laid an iron bar fence. It seemed as if it came down on him in some way. As he lay there, an old drug addict came and started to take off a gold chain the young man had around his neck.

The young man again moaned as if wanting to stop the addict from taking his chain. But it was useless, the old addict told him "Relax *papi*, *yo te conozco*," "I know you man. I'm going to take it and keep it safe for you." Even as a kid I knew something was wrong with this scenario. It literally bothered to see someone take advantage of a person instead of helping. He was not a friend; it was just an addict robbing someone in plain sight. This was the ghetto, where corruption and poverty reigned. What could a person expect in an environment like this one?

I had even saw a daughter once ask her father to lend her his knife for a friend to use. "*Papi*, give me your knife that John needs it. He asked me to tell you to let him borrow it." Her father looked firmly at her and said, "Make sure he takes care of it. And you, better bring it back." Seeing this I thought to myself, "He cares more about his knife than he does about his daughter."

On another afternoon at 3:00 p.m. as I walked out of the school building towards the sidewalk, where parents and older siblings wait to pick up their children. I saw two older boys, holding one of my classmates by his arms. One had his left arm, the other held his right arm. I thought to myself, "What happened here?" But as I walked towards their way to reach the sidewalk, they through him on me. We immediately started fighting, no questions asked. It was winter and I was wearing a big black hairy coat; it looked as if I was wearing a bear. I could hardly move because of the coat, so I took it off and we continued fighting.

But then I could see from the corner of my eyes people grapping at my bookbag and coat. So, in between fighting I also had to protect my property.

What had this fight been about? I did not know; I did know that at times I had fights in school with other kids and we use to tease each other. I also knew I never stood quiet when someone said something to me and I never stood hit. Just as I did not stay hit in this fight I just had. I also do not remember ever going home to complain to my mother or father about fighting in school.

Home had its own ups and downs, at this time our father still lived with us. He worked hard Monday through Friday, for these reasons we barely saw him during the week. He would leave early in the morning and return late in the evenings. Once home, he would shower, eat and go to sleep. At times he would stay up late watching the baseball game. I remember because he would invite me to watch the games with him. "Come sit down and watch the games." He had a style of demanding, instead of asking.

I liked to watch the games with my father. Although he barely spoke, it was to me, a form of bonding. I also liked that the games were quiet most of the time. I could hear the man in the television announcing "one ball, two strikes," in a low voice. Playing, were either the Yankees' game or the Mets. He did not watch any other team play.

My father was tough, old school. He was short and muscular. In his teen years he was a boxer, according to my uncles he was a good fighter too. On Saturdays, my father would give my younger brother Richard and me boxing lessons. He would take us aside a few minutes each and teach us how to stand, put our hands up, move, jab. I remember once asking him to bend down some, so I could reach his face. He did as I said, and I punched him in the mouth and busted his lip.

Other Saturdays my father, would take Richard and me to Central Park. While my mother would take Danny and Evelyn to visit our grandmother in the Low East Side. Danny and Evelyn were my mother's first children which she had with her first husband Daniel. My mother always hint that Daniel was her true love by the way she spoke about him.

One day my brother Richard and I drove our mother crazy. "These two were very disrespectful today!" "They would not listen to me!" Our mom said loudly in Spanish to our father. This was as soon as he walked in through the door. Richard and me had been jumping on a sofa chair our parents had in their room. When mom told us to stop, we did not listen to her. I can remember we were extremely awful that day, more than other days.

It was not the first time my mother pointed out my bad behavior. Some days she would tell me to stop cursing, because I had a filthy mouth. I would just curse out of nowhere for no apparent reason. Yet, this time my father just took off his belt and whipped us as if we were wild animals. We screamed, "okay, okay, we wouldn't do it no more please!!!" The pain was terrible, we tried to hide beneath the blankets but it was useless. I even peed on myself because of the pain. "The next time I'll whip you until you piss on yourself!" My father yelled. While I was thinking to myself, "I already did piss on myself." We stood in

8

our room crying. "Mommy, mommy it hurts!" "It hurts so much." But no one came to comfort us. Why did he beat us so hard that day, I don't know?

By Friday it was a whole different story. My mother didn't cook on Fridays, my father always bought a big pizza pie and a big bottle of soda. We enjoy Fridays, my father would bring the treat home and would leave to hang out with his brothers and friends. Once it started getting late though, my mother would get nerves, *"Hay Dios mio ya mismo este viene borracho a pelear."*

My father would come home late on Fridays. Drunk after drinking most of the night. He would start arguing with my mother and at times I can remember him beating her up. In my memory this appeared to be a weekend routine. How many times did it really happened I do not know? But these fights and arguments would eventually cause them to separate. My father leaving caused mix feelings, on one side we were happy because this meant the fighting would stop, but at the same time it was confusing, our father was leaving.

No father, no respect

"I am going out kids, you guys stay here quietly and behave." "Danny is the oldest so he is in charge." Danny himself was a kid, I was not about to listen to him. My mother had girlfriends even when our father lived with us. But once he was gone, she started hanging out with a woman named Carmen. Carmen had a few boyfriends and had way more life experience than my mother would ever have. Carmen invited my mother to hang out in a club around the block from where we lived. When she leaved, I use to think that she was never going to return, I also felt as if she was going to be miles away. "Mommy, please don't leave, don't leave us alone." "It's night time, please don't go!" I would cry and beg her not to go out and leave us alone, but she would leave anyway.

I noticed I was the only one crying and asking her not to leave. By then my baby sisters were born. They were twins: Janet and Genette. The last kids my parents had together. The twins were small, so they were just put to sleep. Richard was two years younger than me, but I don't remember him ever crying. Danny and Evelyn would mock me for crying and tell me to be quiet. After our mother left the apartment I would also leave. I would go to the building across the street and sit on the stairs in front of the building. "Come back George, you can't leave!" I would hear Danny yelling. "I'm going to tell mom when she comes back." "I don't care, tell her, I'm leaving anyway!" This happened a few times. I didn't care for a beating from my mom, all I care was feeling safer in the streets. How could my mother leave us alone at night to go dancing? She knew these buildings had caught fire on prior occasions.

I saw myself being carried high by many hands; I was in the body of a baby. The crowd just lift me up high and passed me on, from one pair of hands to another. "Mom, dad, where are you?" "We are here sweetheart, but you are not our kid anymore." "We are trading you in for a better baby, even though he is a crippled child." "No, mom, dad, no, no!" "Wake up, wake up,

10

you are dreaming!" "Ma, it was a dream?" "*Si, tranquilo*." "Ma, what happens when we die?" "Is there an afterlife?" "Well, some people say we can come back as a plant, an animal of some sort or maybe in another family." "How about the exact same family, can that happen too?" "Well, you would have to pray and ask God, maybe he can make it happen."

For some reason I started having these nightmares. My parents were still together and they trade me in for a disformed baby. In the dream the crippled baby knew it and mocked me for it. I was also concern about afterlife and the family staying together forever. When my mother told me God could make it happen if I asked him, that I did. I remember running into my room and praying, "God, please, when we die and come back let us be the same family again, please." For me, the breaking up of the family was a tragedy.

Things seem to change in the neighborhood too. When my father still lived at home, neighbors respected us. Once my father left, the respect was gone too. One day, a woman that lived across the street from us invited my mother out to fight. The lady was known for being a troublemaker. I thought my mother would just ignore her, but mom said she had to confront her. I can remember my mother even took a knife with her. I was scared for my mom's life. I asked her not to go out. Mom, said that if she backs down the lady would never respect her.

Mom, went out to talk with the woman. My mother's sister Teresa, who lived upstairs from us, went with her. They were out for a while, it seemed like forever. We were looking out the window and could see them talking. I was scared, I thought my mom would be murdered and never return. Even though nothing happened, emotionally I felt as if she died.

Concourse Plaza

Flames blazed through the windows of the apartments; thick black smoke burst up into the skies above. People were screaming in English and Spanish for people to get out of the builds. "Fire, fire, everybody out!" "¡fuego, fuego, salgan, avanza!" "¡Y los nenes, busca los nenes!" Suddenly, the lights went out in our whole side of the block and we were in the middle of a blackout. Had it not been for the lights of the firetrucks, ambulance and police cars flashing we would have been in total darkness. These buildings had caught on fire before, but people were able to move back into them after some fixing up. But this time they were totally destroyed as many other tenant buildings had been in the Bronx.

The Red Cross also came to our aid; families were moved and placed that very night in the Grand Concourse Plaza Hotel that stood on 161st Street and Grand Concourse. People knew from prior experiences that if the families stayed in the hotel, under the government's help, they would be placed into housing projects. As kids, we were glad. After the fear past, there was some feelings of excitement. We knew we were going to be replaced. That meant leaving this old violent neighborhood.

Grand Concourse was nice. It was quiet and clean. We weren't in the ghetto anymore. The streets were bigger, the blocks looked longer. And there were barely people outside. My mother expressed at times she did not like the neighborhood because it was too quiet. In fact, there were no *bodegas* around. You had to walk far and long to find a store.

In the Hotel, we were still around the same neighbors and friends from Willis Avenue. My aunt Teresa was also living there with her husband and children. Everybody seemed to be happy and even making new friends that were also living in the hotel from other neighborhoods.

At night, my mother would go to one of her girlfriends' apartment. There other ladies from Willies Ave would meet and they played bingo for nickels and dimes. In these hangouts she met a man named Sammy, who became some sort of "boyfriend" to her. Sammy was a skinny, black Puerto Rican man. Sammy had a Puerto Rican homeboy which wore a big afro. He also like to act crazy; they both carried knives and told war stories to the women to impress them. The ladies loved to hear the stories these two guys told them. You could see it in the twinkle of their eyes. And hear it in their giggles as if they were fourteen-year-olds falling in love all over again.

On school days us kids had to travel back to Willis Ave. to attend our classes. At three o'clock our mother would pick us up. On one of these days' mom did not show to pick us up. My siblings and I waited and waited, but she did not arrive. It seemed like forever, and it was very cold outside. I started to worry. We

13

then went across the street to a *bodega* we were familiar with to warm up.

An employee notice that we were alone. "Hey, you kids are waiting for someone to pick you up?" We did not answer him, so he continued, "Who you guys waiting for, your mother?" "She hasn't come yet uh, maybe she has abandoned you guys. That happens a lot, mothers just get tired of their kids and abandon them." Then he started laughing. When I heard him say our mother abandon us, I started to cry, and the man continued to laugh louder. Another man in the *bodega* I interpret to be the boss told the employee to leave us kids alone.

At around five o'clock that evening, our mother showed up saying how sorry she was for not picking us up herself. She explained that she had sent her new boyfriend, Sammy, to pick us up. Oh, she was furious she exclaims. She promised she would not speak to him anymore. *"¡No le hablo más! En casa no lo quiero!"*

Hours later Sammy came to the apartment and mom let him in. At the same time pretending to be upset at him. Meantime he hugged her and told her how sorry he was for not remembering to pick us up from school that day. *"Perdon mi amor*, it won't happen again I promise."

I thought my mother was a fool for trusting this Sammy guy she had just met. I saw her as a coward and a weak woman. Deep inside I started to hate her very much. I then remembered a time back in Willies Ave. when I argued with a boy in the streets and he yelled at me "your mother!" Because I cursed at him. Instantly, in that moment I realized I had no love for the woman that use to leave me alone at night to go dancing at the club with her friend Carmen. I knew I had no love for her because I felt no offence at the boy. I was plain, no feeling, but I yelled back at the boy. "Your mother!" Not to defend my mother, but my own honor. Because I knew that in the streets if you did not defend yourself in someway you would be a victim.

After the day in which Sammy did not pick us up, my mother never took us to school in Willies again. We would miss about a semester from school while in Grand Concourse. After quite a few months of living in the hotel, families were placed in different housing projects. My Aunt Teresa and her kids were sent to housing projects near Willis Ave. Our family was moved to housing projects further uptown, in the Bronx.

One afternoon, our mother informed us that we were given an apartment in the projects. She also explained she had already gone to see the apartment. Then she added, "There is only one thing." When we asked what the one thing was. She answered, "*El vecindario es de morenos.*" She continued, "I don't want to live around Puerto Ricans any more, they like to gossip too much and to get in your life." As kids living among blacks or Puerto Ricans, did not matter to us. I had black friends in my old school and had some black friends that were adults down the block in Willies Ave. which I would always stop by and say hi too. What we did not know was, this new neighborhood had real gangsters living in it. It was one of the toughest neighborhoods in the South Bronx at the time.

Chapter 2

MOVING TO THE NINE

THE YEAR WAS 1972, THE NEIGHBORHOOD was The Clermont Projects, located between 3rd Avenue and Washington Ave. on 169th Street, better known as "The Nine," for a crew that took the name from the last street number in the "169." These were tough times, in a very tough and violent neighborhood. Across the street from the project building where we had just move into, was Junior High School I.S. 148. Its schoolyard had become the turf of two violent gangs—The Savage Skulls and the Ghetto Brothers. I had seen violence in Willis Avenue, but in this new neighborhood the schoolyard was the gang's hang out and the street corner was another crew's hang out. And once a group hanged out in any territory, that area was considered their turf. No other group could come in and claim it. If you did not live in the neighborhood, but you had to walk through the neighborhood, it was best if you walked through it with respect.

Besides the gangs or crews, the people here were just as violent and aggressive. One day going up in the elevator to our new apartment. My mother and us kids, as usual. I guess to people we seem like the mother hen with her chicks. In the elevator with us, there were three young black men. They were speaking among themselves and laughing; the elevator stopped and they started to get off on their floor. As the door went to close my mother said to them, "what is so funny?" Before the door completely close, a hand grabbed the elevator door and pushed it back open. It was the biggest and tallest guy of the group. He asked my mother firmly, "What you say lady?" I could see in my mother's facial expression she was afraid. "Nothing. I just asked what is so funny." She told him with her noticeable Puerto Rican accent. "Be careful lady on how you speak." I was more surprised than scare, I could see the man's intention of wanting to hit my mother, not caring that she was a woman and had children with her.

Church

Almost immediately after moving to this new neighborhood my mother started going to a Pentecostal Church named '*Los Ciento Veinte*' meaning 120 in English. For the number of those present when the Apostle Peter spoke for the electing of Matthias in Acts 1:15.

The church was located in Brook Avenue, not too far from where we lived. At times, we would walk to the church; other times we would wait for the church van to pick us up. It was a small store front church. It appeared as if the whole thing was made out of wood with a cement foundation. Inside, it had big purple curtains that looked like flags on each side of the walls. At times the lights were dim, and it made it look like a funeral home.

The pastor Jesus Suarez, the founder of the church and many of its members were Puerto Rican migrants that came to the U.S. mainland sometime in the 1950s. The majority of the congregation were related to each other, including the pastor. The pastor appeared to be old, maybe older than what he really was. His hair was very white, so white it seemed to shine. He was the patriarch, but also a *jibarito* with no education (a *jibarito* is a person that lives in the countryside of Puerto Rico, and is regarded as lacking intelligence) not even in theology. But he felt his vocation to preach the word of God.

He screamed a lot when he preached, and interpret the bible as a layman would. He criticized preachers that prepared their sermons and used outlines to preach their message. Sometime that was all his message was, a criticism to someone or something. But when you knew him in a personal level, he was a nice old man.

He had a brother named Erasmo Suarez. Erasmo was an Elder in the church; he too appeared to be very old, also with white shiny hair, but a very friendly and nice old man. Erasmo had quite a few sons and daughters but they were all grown and married. Except for one of his boys that happened to be around my age. Somewhere around nine or ten years of age. His name Benji. For some reason I did not like even the looks of him. I thought he looked like an old man too. He was very proud, maybe a cover up for being lonely and having a father that appear to be his grandfather I thought.

My brother Richard and I would always pick on him. And if he got out of hand, we would slap him or punch him in the face. His older sister Gladys (she had the same name as my mother) would come to his defense. If not, it would be his uncle Jose. This set us in a bad start with the people of the church. Every time something wrong happened, I would get the blame. And I was not the type to go down quiet, I would fight in my defense.

The pastor also had an older son named Moses, who was the guitar player. Married and with just two kids at the time. Moses seem cool, I got along with him. He knew how to treat us well. He was an unarmed police officer in the welfare department.

While this family could have been considered an oligarchy, I believed we were considered outsiders. My mother was a single parent with six kids. I did not see it then, but she was young, she couldn't be no more than thirty years old. And she had no control over us, so she let us do what we wanted I realize.

I got in constant trouble, fighting even with the adults. There were times when I was even hit by some of the adult males. At another time, I was slapped by two adults. I would fight back but I was just a kid. The most I could do was curse, scream, and tell the people I hated them. Some adult would tell me, "you don't appreciate it now, but when you grow up you will." I would yell all the more, "no I won't, they are not my father!"

I would tell myself that if my father was present, they would not hit me, but the fact was, my father was not present. On top of that, I had to face the fact that my mother would not defend me. Most of the time, when I got into an argument or any type of confrontation, she was present but did nothing. On occasions, she would tell me, "If someone hit you, it's because you did something wrong." "But they are not my father!" I would get so upset, I felt at times I could not breath. I tell myself "she was not my mother; she is just a woman I live with." There were also moments she would tell me I remind her of my father. Still, this church would become part of our weekly activities and my mother's social life.

My Mother

My mother's name was Gladys, she was one of seven children born to her parents. They came from the island of Puerto Rico to New York City in the late 1950s. She was approximately fifteen years of age when she arrived to New York. By seventeen she would be married and giving birth to her first born, my oldest brother Danny. When that marriage did not work out my mother separated from her first husband but never divorced him. Sometimes it seemed as if she had hopes that he would come back.

She then met my father who she had four kids by, me being the oldest and the twins the youngest. But now she was single again, but with six kids. We were not easy, we fought each other often. Most of the time Danny started the disputes. Maybe by playing in silly ways but things would spin out of hand and a fight would always start.

In other occasions Danny would start fight with us on purpose, either way it did not matter. I know that with time I started to hate him. I also hated the fact that my mother enabled the bullying that went on by not doing nothing about it. She put no order, and at times made excuses for him by telling us that he just wanted to play, but the bullying was real.

In other occasions the fights were between Danny and Evelyn. Sometimes violent and with blood shed. Still my mother did nothing except blame Evelyn for starting. Even if Evelyn didn't start the fight. I was well aware of the injustice. I notice my mother took Danny's side always and discriminated against her three girls. As if the female meant nothing to her.

I would hear her speak about women as if they were less than men. I truly could not believe the things I would hear her say about women, maybe she was reflecting on herself. She had no inspiration to do better in life. Even when I use to tell her "when I grow up, I want to be a police officer." She would tell me "you wouldn't be able to be a police officer; you are going to be to short." Then she would have saying like "once your born in the pit, you die in the pit."

I would tell myself "don't listen to her, that's not true. Life is what you make of it." "If you want to do good you can do good, don't listen to her." But still because of her new religious believes and the legalistic teachings in the church. Once she discovered gangs attract my attention, *I became El hijo del diablo* to her.

How hurtful it was to hear her call me that. It was constant, it last for a short time, but constant. When that wasn't the case it was her telling me to go to my room with the demons where I belong. She never forced me to do so, but just saying the words

21

cause me to panic. Enough to scream and cry out loud as if I was being beaten.

Fights among us went on until our early teen years, then they stopped. Richard and I started working out very young. We came from good genes, my father was a boxer, and his brother a body-builder and all their siblings were naturally short and muscular. This started showing on Richard and me at a young age.

In time we learned Danny was having trouble in school and I would ask him, "why don't you fight back or make friends with the kids your age?" He would give me excuses I did not buy into. The truth was we were getting older and things were changing. I learn violence was a solution. My father left; I did not have an older brother I could look up too. That left me being the man of the house, you couldn't tell me I wasn't an adult at thirteen. Even though I wasn't one, I thought I was.

School

When we arrived to the new neighborhood, I remember we missed a semester of class, so we started school in the month of January. I was in the third grade; our teacher was a very short, elderly, Jewish woman. It was said that she had been in a German concentration camp. Secretly, I admired that she had been part of history. To get to the elementary school we had to cross the street, pass I.S. 148. Walk a block up the hill, turn left at the corner and then we would reach P.S. # 2.

Being that this school was in a predominantly black neighborhood, the students were mainly black. There were only about two or maybe three students that were of Puerto Rican descendant in the classroom. This school was also a violent place. Our schoolyard looked down into the I.S. 148 schoolyard. We could see everything that the older kids did. We could see the real gangs, with their gang jackets and combat boots. It was an attractive sight to us kids.

Fights would break out every day in I.S. 148. Even stabbings or slashings and we would watch with awe. Many of the kids in P.S. 2, had older brothers that had been in prison. So, when a teacher called a student's attention, the teacher had to be mindful of the possibility of the student having a brother that was a gang member or an ex-con.

The students formed small groups and imitated the real gangs. We even fought other kids at lunchtime from other schools that were not far from our school. But before I could be accepted into a group, I had to prove myself. This was not a gang initiation; it was just that the new comers were picked on. And you either fought back or get pick on every day.

I remember my first fight. It was with Michael Timmins. We were going to class and I heard him tell other kids in the class line while in the hallway, "once we get into the classroom, I am going to hit me." I knew never to stay hit. When we got into the classroom Michael hit me. I hit him back and he grabbed me by the neck with his arm. He was taller than me and had long arms, but I just punched all over his body with both arms.

"Fight, fight! Get him Mike, yo, that new kid is fighting back man!" The fight was finally stop and Michael never bothered me again. In fact, we became friends and I started making more friends. The catch was that now I was part of the crew. So, there would be other fights; the only difference now was I had some backup. But being part of a group, meant that I had to be up to breaking into supply rooms, fighting against other group of kids and at times cut class.

The first time I was asked if I was down to fight against a group from another school, I was honored. I said yes immediately, and those that asked me were glad I said yes. They did not just ask me, they went around asking other kids too, as if recruiting them. Those that said yes were well off. The ones that said no out of fear would be target and could be picked on at any time. In fact, the kids that said no were being jumped and beaten up for the next few days.

There was a teacher which got upset every time she saw me. It was as if my presence alone bothered her. She was aggressive towards me, and did not care to hide it. I notice this and did not like her either. It came to the point where even the sound of her voice bothered me.

One day, during a routine class work, where the teacher handout a sheet with similar words in boxes. She would call out a word and the students had to circle the correct word. She noticed I was lost and confused. She immediately got up, stood over me and asked me. "George, what word are we on?" I looked up and saw this giant human being standing over me, with such a threatening body language. I did not say a word, I felt threaten and shamed. Plus, I did not know what word we were on. They all looked the same to me.

The teacher then raised her voice so loud in front of the classroom and yell, "George, do you know where you are going to be next year? In the third grade, the third grade!!!" I said nothing but just sunk into my chair, while feeling all eyes on me. From that moment on reading and spelling became my boogeyman.

Once three o'clock came the teacher gave my mother an envelope with a note informing her that I would be repeating third grade for the following year. My mother was very upset at me, but never ask why her child was being held back. I thought to myself, "you never study with me, nor do you supervise my homework."

One afternoon, while we were still in classroom, we heard sirens in the streets zooming by, it seemed as if this went on for thirty minutes or more. We knew something happened and it couldn't be good. Once out of school we saw people running down the street to a corner store; someone had been shot. I ran to see what happened; once there I pushed in through the crowd and saw lying in front of me, a dead man. Although he was covered with a white sheet. I could see blood on the sidewalk next to his head and a cigarette near him.

It was said by bystanders that two armed robbers came out running after robbing the store at gun point. The dead man was walking on the sidewalk with his daughter in his arms. One of the robbers bumped into the man. His gun pointed up to the man's face. The man's reflex caused him to immediately grab the gun and the robber shot him just as fast. Leaving the man dead in front of his daughter; lying there with blood gushing from his head. The sight and the information given by the people, penetrated into my mind; this image would stay with me for a long time. I felt as if life was cheap—one minute a person is here and the next he is gone.

The Neighborhood

The Nine was a lively neighborhood, in the summer people were outside 24/7. Music was constantly playing from some apartment, car, or radio. I used to stay up late at night as a kid and in the weekends, I would get up early. I use to do this to look out the window and see what was going on. I saw fights or guys challenging each other. These guys were really tough, they were real. Thugs with gangster reputations, we were in a real tough neighborhood. I felt my mother was happy here she did not want to move. For us kids we, were happy too. We felt safe from all the fires we had experienced in Willie Ave. but some events would cause me to want to move.

One night, while we were watching television, my mother was looking out the window and she started scream *"Dios mio, Dios mio!"* We jumped and ran to the window, "What happened?" She started to tell us, she witnessed some guys playing basketball across the street and other guys came into the basketball court with baseball bats and started swinging the bats on the guys playing ball, then they immediately disappeared just as fast as they came in, jumping over the small fence that was around the basketball court. I was impressed with the story and upset with myself at the same time for missing the action. "Next time something happens I want to see it."

One night, as we waited for the church van to pick us up for church, I got my wish to see some action. We were standing right by the corner store on 169th Street and Washington Avenue and again my mother screamed. I turned around and saw three young black men running out the store with a gun in hand.

I got scared and wanted to run into a nearby barbershop. "Mom let's go in here." I remember walking ahead of my mother. She told me "No, they left; the van will be here to pick us up soon." I was scared and thought she was crazy for staying outside waiting for the van instead of taking cover in one of the opened businesses.

After that up-close event I wanted out of the neighborhood and I would constantly ask my mother to move from the projects. Every time I would see a FOR RENT sign, I would tell my mother to take the number down. My mother would say yes, but never did call any of the numbers. The projects were a safe haven for her—no matter how much violence there was outside, she felt we were safe inside. The violent "9" became our home.

Chapter 3

BEING FOURTEEN

YEARS PAST AND WE WERE OLDER—I WAS fourteen I was sure I was a man. By now I loved the Nine too much to leave it. Now my mother could not get me out of here even if she tried. I started going to I.S. 148 myself. Here, I made new friends. Some of my old friends I did not see at all. There were many new faces, even people who were not from the neighborhood.

The Savage Skulls and the Ghetto Brothers were no longer hanging out in the schoolyard of I.S. 148. How did that happen? I didn't know, but two of my new friends had been members of the baby Ghetto Brothers. Their story use to make me laugh, because they did not volunteer to join the gang or even want to join. They told us they were forced to join. The president of the gang was forcefully recruiting members and he told Scott, one of the two boys telling the story, "You are a new member." Scott said he just agreed and that was it. He was part of the baby ghetto brothers.

I asked Scott, why did he say yes. He told me it was a tough gang and the leader was crazy, so he did not feel he could say no. Plus, they controlled the neighborhood. The other boy was Rey, a Puerto Rican. I understand Rey was also forced into the gang, and that's how they knew each other. We had other homeboys from Webster Avenue in I.S. 148.

Now, historically, some Webster Avenue boys were not welcome on the Nine. Unless they knew someone. So, whenever they came through, they had to come with respect. But Webster Avenue boys weren't punks; they were tough too and, in their history, Webster had some tough gangs in their turf. Gangs like the Casanova, Bachelor, among others.

Some other new friends I made in 148 were Martin which we called Little Mike; he was from 70. 70 was one block up from 169 Street. They took the last two numbers from the 170 of their Street number on their block. Little Mike and I hit it off well, we hanged and knew we had each other's back. Then there was Ruben Peña, which was from Webster Ave. One of the four Peña brothers. His oldest brother had done prison time. In the streets this was always a big deal. There was Eddie, who we called Barnie Rubble because he was stocky. I think a better name for him was Bam-Bam because he was always getting into a fight. One of these friends was Alex Ramos, nicknamed Nano, short for *Enano,* which means "midget" in Spanish, because Alex was very short.

Nano and I knew each other since the third grade, when I first arrived at P.S. 2. It was rough for him back then because, although he was Puerto Rican, he was white and had blond hair. The same went for his older brother Jose, which we called Bucky. But we were older now and Nano, like me, had years living here and we had survived that beginning where we had to fight or be bullied. In this first year of junior high school, these guys were the guys I could count on whether black or Puerto Ricans.

By the eighth grade, our Puerto Rican crew was hanging out with each other, not only in school but also outside of school. Our bond became stronger. Sometimes we had hooky parties, where we cut class and went with some girls to one of the fellow's apartment. Of course, for this their parents had to be working.

Beside the hang out and fun, we also had each other's back if we got into any problems. Which did occur from time to time. There were fights and group fights, at times even among one another. In a case where the fight was among us, we just made sure it would be a fair one on one.

In the course of time I continue to meet some of the older brothers of my new friends. By meeting the fellas, a sense of belonging, protection, and family also grew. Things changed; I was not a little kid anymore. My father's absence did not matter now. In the summer, there were summer job programs for teens. I believe to keep adolescence busy and out of trouble.

Although, this was not the first time I ever worked. Chiro, my aunt Teresa's husband would take me with him at times to do pluming and soldering since I was about twelve years of age. But with the summer job it was better work and pay. We did not have to go through the hard times we did as kids. I was making my own money, no matter the amount. I didn't have bills to pay no how. Plus, I was staying busy even if it was only for the summer.

I even started to go to church on my own, because I wanted too. It turned out to be a good experience for me, I believed it help me mature some and I had a personal spiritual experience with God in my faith. Plus, I was older, no one was going to hit me as it happened when I was a kid.

By now the church moved from location; they had a new building up in Morris Avenue between 169th Street and 170th Street. The new building was bigger and brighter than the old building had been. New families came in and a lot of the old families moved away, some back to Puerto Rico. The oligarchy appeared to have ceased.

The pastor was still the same elderly man who continued his screaming when he preached. The pastor's son still played the guitar and would become the youth Sunday School teacher. I can say he tried to reach out to us youth and to me in specific. Something that deep inside of me I appreciated.

In this bigger church at the new location, a man we would know as Mr. Cruz, started visiting. He had a son named Audie Cruz. Audie and I bond almost immediately, Audie told me he had been a member of the Latin Seven. I shared my street experience with him. But we hit it off mainly because we both were into working out. Audie asked me if I did any jogging besides lifting weights. When I told him I did not, he challenge me and that was the beginning of me adding running to my workout routine.

We all loved Mr. Cruz and everyone called him *Papi* Cruz— everyone except me. I tried but the word *papi* was not coming out of my mouth. I had no father, that was blocked out and no one could substitute that emptiness. Audie told me his dad had been a Young Lord. That was impressive to know, Mr. Cruz was also a community leader and a person that stood up for what he believed in. Mr. Cruz gave his all for the youth of the church and helped us find jobs in the Summer.

Yet, after about a year and a half and a lot of good experiences, I decided to stop going to church. There was always the ups and downs at home and the temptation of the youth life. I also saw and knew about a lot of serious problems in the church.

Plus, the streets, the homeboys and neighborhood were attracting me too much and I wanted to do what I wanted. By then, I had also dropped out of school and felt I had failed. I might as well go hang out with others that were in my own shoes and were not thinking about school. Who thinks about school in the street corners? So, that I did.

Teen years: In Need of a Role Model

It was now 1980 and although I worked for a little while in Mr. Rivera's *bodega* I would shortly quit that job. I was idle and looking for some action in my life. After I stopped visiting the church, I started getting into fights again. I started hanging out more with the homeboys. We called ourselves The Minor Crew, because we were younger than the older homeboys. We had each other's back.

Little Mike

One day, Little Mike told me and the rest of the Minor Crew he was having some trouble uptown in his girlfriend's block. He knew we had his back, as we always did with each other. Although it was a bit difficult because this was his girlfriend's neighborhood. It was somebody else's turf and he would have to go back if he wanted to see his girl.

Either way, we got the fellas together, the Minor Crew and the older fellas. We needed them. They had the cars and guns, Mike warned us to just watch his back. So, we did as he asked. We went uptown with him to have his back but knowing we couldn't go crazy on anyone unless it was necessary.

The fellas that came with us from the older crew was Speedy, the slickest and most sharp dress Puerto Rican you could meet. Everyone knew him and loved, both blacks and Puerto Ricans, but you couldn't sleep on him. Then there was Big Nest (short for Nestor) he had just come home from doing a year and a half up in the state prison, but he was not going to let us go without his support. Between both crew we had a nice number of fellas.

We set up a plan to trap the guys that were starting the trouble with Mike. The Minor Crew, would walk in the building with Mike ahead of the older fellas which were not even insight. We knew this would provoke the crew from that neighborhood to come after us and it worked.

The crew from Mike's girl's neighborhood saw us go in the building and they came in after us. As they followed behind us,

33

they were taking off their belts from their waist. We went up the stairs as if we did not know we were being followed. Yet, we were doing the same thing. Taking off our belts to fight with our belt buckles. At the same time, we were pulling out our knives. The crew from that block came in the building, and we started back down the stairs towards them. But up from behind them came our back up with their guns drawn, we had their crew trapped in the middle. Had Mike not told us to play it cool from the beginning, the lobby would have turned into a bloodbath.

Still blood was shed, but only because of the fistfight that followed. After Mike and the guy that was starting most of the trouble slugged it out, one of the older fellas, Edgar threw his arm around Mike's shoulders and warned, "if we have to come back, it's not going to be for a fistfight, and there won't be no talking neither." As we drove back to the Nine, we laughed and bragged about how cool the older fellas looked coming up from behind with guns in hand. "man, if only Mike didn't have to go back, we could have just lit them up."

Once we got back on the Nine, we thanked Speed, Nest, and the rest of the older fellas for having our backs. A few days later, Nest asked me for a solid. It would be my pleasure I thought. Ruben and I returned the favor for Nest and took care of some young punk that got disrespectful with Nest. Nest did not want to hurt the kid because he was younger than Nest. Plus, Nest was on parole. So, we took care of it for him. This is the way it was, if anyone messed with any of us—we would get to them one way or another.

The Nine was a family with in itself. If you lived here, we could not allow an outsider to come in to hurt any of us, it was just the law in our streets. For a person to get a fair fight here, you had to live in the neighborhood. In the summertime, we had block parties and many people got into fights. If you were an outsider, you would be jumped, stomped, and robbed. Sometimes, we would jump outsiders for just coming into our neighborhood, even if they came in peace. It all depended on how we felt.

On other occasions, we went into other neighborhoods that we knew were having block parties. We would enjoy the music and dance until the D.J. would announce that the next song coming on was the last song of the night. Then our crew would start snatching chains off people's necks. Punching people in the face. It was dangerous, because we were not in our block. This one particular night we were in the Forest Hills Project in a block party.

What saved us was that people would push into each other and numerous fights broke out. Plus, I had made friends with some guys from Webster Avenue which I had told whenever they came on the Nine, to ask for me. I would do the same when I went to Webster. Uniting our crews gave us strength. This night we got together. My Webster crew and some of the fellas from the Nine.

As we were leaving the block party after starting the chaos, one of our guys looked back and warned us that a group of guys was following us. I clutched my twelve-inch knife I had in my waist. One of my guys, we called Put, yelled to me. Telling me not to leave him. Put was limping because of a burglary we did the night before, where we both had to jump out a window to get away. I waited for Put to go on ahead of me. I assured him I would not leave him.

The guys following us made the mistake of following us back to the Nine. Once we were in our neighborhood, I yelled out, "Nine Crew!" The four corners of our block were full. All the homeboys were out that night. Once I called out the fellas came up to me asking what was up. Everyone could see the other guys coming down the block towards us. I told the fellas how we had just finished robbing them in their own neighborhood. But before we knew it, the guys following us were on top of us claiming their gold chains back. Some of them still had big gold chains around their neck. So, we proceed to finish in our block what we started in their neighborhood. In an instant we stripping them of their gold and beating them out of our neighborhood. We watched them run out quicker than they came in.

Chapter 4

DEATH OF A HOMEBOY

I HAD ANOTHER HOMEBOY ON THE NINE. People called him Peanut or Nut for short. He was one of the Timmons brothers. He was known for being violent, or crazy as some would say about him. I saw him slap a woman hard in the face, in front of her husband for staring at him. But to me, Nut was a big brother. When he learned my name was George, Nut told me, "From now on I'm calling you Baby-G." Nut let me know he had two sawed-off shotguns and a .38 Smith and Wesson. He also told me if I ever needed them to let him know. But he warned me not to do anything that was unnecessary.

Beside wild and aggressive as Peanut was, he was also a hustler. A hustler is what we call brothers who knew how to make money. He hustled right on the Nine. Nut was one of six brothers. To my surprise his oldest brother was a minister for the Seventh-day Adventist Church. Yet, three of his other brothers were in prison for violent crimes. They were the notorious Timmons brothers. Nut himself had been in federal prison.

Now Nut had a younger brother he called Ju-Ju. Ju-Ju was around sixteen years old and very wild. Ju-Ju lived with his mother in Queens, where she had moved to. She left 70, where she lived in the Bronx wanting to give Ju-Ju a better life. But being that Nut lived in the Bronx, Ju-Ju would come and visit him. Ju-Ju looked up to Peanut. Nut always had money and had the corner where he made his money under control.

Nut and I hit it off well and we became inseparable. I started to go with Nut to Harlem to watch his back when he did business. At times I would take some Puerto Rican homeboys with me to have more protection. These were times when people couldn't just go into Harlem, especially to the areas we walked into. Because we were Puerto Ricans it was easy to notice us. Traditionally Puerto Ricans in Harlem are on East Harlem. We went into the Westside of Harlem, which was the Afro American side of Harlem. After sometime when we went out there and the dealers saw us. They knew it was Nut and his Puerto Rican crew.

By 1982, I started to get the idea of going to the army and getting away from the Nine. I told Nut about my idea of going to the army and he told me, "Man, you're crazy, the army is just like prison." When Ju-Ju heard Nut tell me the army was like prison, he did not agree with him. Ju-Ju told me, "Man, you are thinking right. One day, we're both going to join the army." I was surprised to hear Ju-Ju speak like that; I guess I was not the only one that wanted out of the dead-end neighborhood.

Out in Queens Ju-Ju started getting in trouble, constantly getting into fights. Nut was worried for his little brother. At times, Nut gathered a few of us fellas to go out to Queens to see what problems Ju-Ju was having and to back him up. But every time we got to Queens from the Bronx Ju-Ju was already sound asleep from all the drinking he had done. A short time after those incidents, I got to the block and Nut came up to me with tears in his eyes and told me Ju-Ju was in a coma.

Ju-Ju had gotten into a fight with some guy out in Queens and the guy's brother ran up behind Ju-Ju with a baseball bat and struck Ju-Ju in the back of the head. Then they both kicked and stomped Ju-Ju into a coma. Ju-Ju died about a week later in the hospital.

We then heard that some of the homeboys of the two guys that killed Ju-Ju came and watched them stomp Ju-Ju. One of the guys watching, robbed Ju-Ju of his sneakers as he lied unconscious. After a few weeks passed and we had mourned Ju-Ju, it was time to get back at anybody who had anything to do with Ju-Ju's death. One night, Nut and I strapped up with a .38 S&W and a .22 revolver. We went off to Jamaica Queens by ourselves.

I had the .38 S&W; Nut had the .22 revolver in the front pocket of his jeans. We got to the neighborhood of Ju-Ju's friend. This friend had been with Ju-Ju the night he got jumped. But he did not help Ju-Ju. In fact, he ran, leaving Ju-Ju alone. I wanted to find this so-called friend, just as bad as I wanted to find those that killed him. But we did not find no one that day.

Nut Goes to Jail

Peanut liked to dress up, there were times when he would come to the block in a three-piece suit. He wore his velour

39

gangster hat tilt to the side. One night, he set out to go to Queens with his wife Rainy and his little boy Barry. I saw him right before he left. I was with a good homeboy the fellas called Big George. People called him Big George to distinguish him from me. Being that we both are named George, but he is much taller than me. Big George and I were going to play pool in Webster Avenue.

"Nut, what's up man?"

"I'm going to Queens."

"Your gonna take care of business?"

"No man, I'm chilling."

"Nut, if you plan on taking care of business let me know I'll go with you."

"No, that's my word. I don't plan on doing nothing; when I do, I'll let you know."

"Cool. I'll go with you then."

Nut headed off to Queens with his wife and kid. I continued to Webster Avenue with Big George. We hung out in the pool hall for a few hours, which was something we did from time to time. The next day, I did not see Nut. I thought he was just staying off the block for a day or two. After a few days went by, I got in touch with his Rainy. When she saw me, she immediately told me she has been wanting to see me. "Nut has been arrested for shooting some guy in Queens. He is in Riker's Island as we speak." Rainy was furious with Nut and the whole situation that was going on. She was tired of the life style she had been living with him. "I am tired of the violence, his drug dealing, arrests, all these problems with the police and courts." She continued, "I was not raised like

40

this." She then told me the cops asked her, "Does your husband always wear a three-piece suit when he goes to shoot somebody?"

On the night of the shooting, after Nut shot at the guys, hitting one of them. He then went back to his mother's house and sat on a chair on the porch of the house. Never took the suit off, just sat there. Rainy explain these things to me in details, but I had to go see Peanut and hear all the detail from him.

So, I went to visit Nut at Riker's Island and asked him what went down. "I thought you weren't going to do nothing Nut, what happened?" "I wasn't going to do nothing. The guys that killed my brother had already been were arrested. There was no reason for me to do something. But then, a friend of Ju-Ju's told me that the guy that took Ju-Ju's sneakers was around. So, I went to where he was just to question him about what happened that night with Ju-Ju and the sneakers. When I asked him why he took my brother's sneakers, he smiled and said, Ju-Ju told me to take them. I thought to myself cool and turned around and just started to walk away. But then it hit me. How could Ju-Ju ask him to take his sneakers if he was out? Then the guy's smile just kept on flashing in my head. I got so full of rage man, I just turned around and started shooting at all the guys who were there with him and I hit him, I shot him in the back as he ran like a coward."

The guy shot was the one who like a coward had taken Ju-Ju's sneakers while Ju-Ju laid unconscious on the cold sidewalk. He was shot in the lower back and became paralyzed. Now, Nut was in prison and facing some serious charges of an attempt murder. I wanted to see Nut home not in prison; this was Nut, my homeboy.

41

I believed I could truly help him in some way beat this attempt murder charge. I called another homeboy, Nut's brother-in-law, Terrence, and told him that we had to get Nut out. We started planning what to do.

On a few occasions, we went by the victim's house to see if we would find him outside. We planned to put a gun to his head and threaten him to drop the charges or change the statement made against Nut. But we never found him outside. Being that he was paralyzed if he had been outside, it would most likely be in a wheelchair and with someone. So, we then got the guys phone number and made threats by phone. The guy would cry and say he was going to change the statement, but what he really was doing was going to the District Attorney telling him that Nut's homeboys were making threatening phone calls.

The threats hurt Nut's case because the courts would not, by any means lower Nut's bail. Nut had beaten other case and we would always have him back on the block. This time it did not go well for him. Nut would eventually be sentenced to five to ten years in prison for attempt murder.

Armed Robberies and Other Hustles

One night, while out on the Nine, and thinking to myself "I want to make a quick dollar, but I need a gun." This urge I felt to rob someone at gunpoint was like a hunger I felt within me. A few minutes later, my homeboy Life came around. "Yo, what's up Baby G?" "Ain't nothing. Life. I'm just think on getting paid, but I don't want to use my hands. I want to stick something up." Stick-up is what we called armed robberies. Life smile and asked. "You serious my brother, because look what I got." He opened his leather jacket and showed me a 9-millimeter gun he was carrying in his waist. When I saw the gun, I yelled "Jackpot!" Immediately we were off in search for a drug dealer. It was night, who else could have money on them but a drug dealer. We started walking. We went up the hill, to Fulton Avenue. We did not see anyone we could rob at gun point. We kept on walking to Boston Road. There we saw some drug dealers on their corner, on their block. Deep inside I knew this was a dumb move. I was to close to home and everyone knew me.

When Life saw the dealers, he wanted to get them. Suddenly, Life recognize one of the dealers from prison and had a change of heart. "No Baby G, we can't do this here; that's my man." He said pointing to one of the guys. "Plus, you're too close to home." Life went up to his homeboy and greeted him, then we realize a brother named Mike that lived in the same building I lived in was among the dealers. We all greeted each other, then me and Life kept moving.

We walked around some more and finally we went into a building we knew had a weed spot on the second floor. We waited down in the first floor for someone to come out. Two guys were coming down the stairs. They had just bought weed. I put on a ski mask I had, after all we were still close to home. Life pulled out the 9-millimeter, we pushed the guys back. We announced it was a stick-up. I patted the guys down quickly. Suddenly, one of the guys said, "I don't know why you are doing this. We don't have no money, plus you live on the Nine." He pointed at me while telling me I live on the Nine.

I could not believe it—he knew who I was even with the ski mask. What do we do now, do we kill these guys for nothing? They didn't even have money on them. Life called out "okay, you guys could leave, go ahead, step off." Then Life told me "I had to let them go. They were broke and they knew who you were." We called it a night and promised we would get together again some other time. This was the beginning of many more armed robberies. And I would have many more stick-up partners in the time to come. Life and I did get together again. We even hit a drug spot, because we knew they had money that could not be reported to the police.

The Nine had a few brothers that were stick up kids. Some claimed to be the best at it. Kenny Harding was one that claimed, not only to be the best, but to have been the teacher of many other gunmen. He was a happy guy; he was always saying jokes. He knew people everywhere he went. And had a girlfriend everywhere he went. He was crazy enough to take out the time to pat a puppy in the middle of an armed robbery. He was crazy, but calm and relaxed. He was not quick to shoot a person. I remember once, we were about to rob a spot at gunpoint. Kenny seeing there was a man with his child. Approached the man and asked him if the police past by often. The man answered no, then Kenny told the man it was best if he leaves because we were about to stick up the place. After a thank you from the man and the exchange of some friendly words the man left. Kenny and I would commit a whole lot of more armed robberies. I have to admit he was quite good and quite the teacher. Never was there any unnecessary violence.

Around this time (in which I was in my stick-up spree) another one of the fellas from the Nine came home from prison. His name was Stephen Harris, he was a 24 years old young man. He was around six feet tall and appeared to be very skinny. Yet because he liked exercising so much, he was very muscular. He served seven and a half years in prison. Stephen had been in and out of juvenile facilities since he was very young. He practically grew up in the system.

Stephen and I started hanging out because we both were into running and hitting the gym. It had nothing to do with committing crimes. Stephen and I did not get high, we did not drink, nor did we smoke. He found out I was going to Jerome Boxing Gym somewhere in a 149th Street and he invited me to go to Grammercy gym with him on 14th Street and 4th Avenue. Where Sargent Jackson, a correctional officer from Sing-Sing Correctional Facility trained ex-inmates which were release. We hit it off, we met almost every morning to run in Macon's Park in the Bronx. Of course, with time the war stories would start between us.

After some weeks past, Stephen told me he wanted me to meet a friend of his. A homeboy from prison. I agreed and Stephen introduced me to a fella who went by the name of Pop. Pop was half Irish and half Portuguese. But he could pass for a Puerto

Rican or black light skin brother. He seemed like an alright guy; Pop too had just come home from serving seven years in prison.

Stephen had a younger brother named Vincent who we called Vinnie for short. Vinnie would go down to Midtown Manhattan to pick pockets with his boys. Stephen started gathering a little crew of about four or five guys and heading out to Midtown to make some money. Although picking pockets was not my thing. I would go out there because Midtown was amazing. It was the 80s and Midtown was changing from what it had been in the 1970s. It was becoming a tourist attraction.

The street life in Midtown was a fast one and at times even dangerous. Even going to Midtown was dangerous. We would take the train early Saturday morning. Stephen would usually pick me at my girlfriend's apartment down in Webster Avenue where I would spend my Friday nights. Once in the train, we would take the last cart where all the hustler and thugs heading to Midtown would be seated. At times fight would breakout. Razors would be drawn, you had to be ready. You had to have a crew, if you were alone you were in trouble.

In Midtown you could not underestimate no one. I saw a couple coming from way down the street. A man and a woman. Both well dressed, suit and tie. The woman had a fancy dress and high heel shoes. They would appear to be drawn in by the hustlers. The couple would play their money and win and then eventually lost. You would think they were victims of these hustlers. But I would later learn that the couple were in on the hustle.

They act interested enough to play their money only to attract other people into playing.

When our crew made money, we would step into some fancy pizza shop, order a pizza pie and some drinks. We then sat down to eat. Then counted the money we made and split it among us. Of course, this was done towards the end of the day. It was here, to my surprise that I saw the well-dressed couple together with the street hustlers splitting money among themselves. I was shocked. I saw a lot of other homeboys from the Nine out here. It seemed as if Midtown was the place to be on Saturdays.

One night while hanging with the youngest of the Alvarez brothers. We would get into some trouble. The Alvarez were a tough family. They were cool, but tough. From the parents even to the girls. People did not want no problem with them.

On this particular night, Raymond Alvarez and I walked into the auditorium of I.S. 148 where a marching band was practicing for an upcoming event. Before entering the school, I notice Raymond picked up a rock he saw in the street. We walked in and sat down. Everyone in there was part of the band in one way or another. The only outsiders there were us. Suddenly Raymond took the rock out of his pocket and threw it to a group of guys sitting in the front row. One of the guys Raymond threw the rock too got up and started looking back. He wanted to see who threw the rock. In that same instant Raymond grabbed a flagpole and threw it at some girls that were also sitting in the front row too but on the opposite side to the boys.

The guy saw Raymond throw the flagpole. He came up to where Raymond and I were sitting. He punched Raymond in the face. Raymond went down and came up laughing. Then he took a swing at me. I ducked in my seat and the guy's fist hit my ear. I got up, put my fist up in a fighting position. The guy put his fist up but he was moving backwards as everyone came in yelling and threatening us. But a man that knew me from the neighborhood jump in between the people and me. He begged the people to stop, yelling to them "please stop, you don't know who you are messing with, please stop!!!" I was surprised at this man's reaction. He looked familiar but I was not sure where I knew him from.

One thing I did know was I had a reputation and people knew about it. I had even shot some guys one night for driving by our neighborhood very slow as if they were looking for one of the fellas. They drove by a few times. I had a sawed-off shotgun hidden among by the garbage dumpster. I pulled it out and ran towards the car and shot. The car crashed into another car. Its glass shattered. As I ran from that incident, one of the homeboys J.G. told me "give me the shotgun and I'll finish them off."

The police were called behind the incident in the auditorium and they came. Raymond and I were still in the area. We were told by the police to leave. I told the officers I would leave, but I also told them I would be back. I let them know it was not over.

The next day Raymond, Life, and me returned with base-ball bats. I attacked swiftly. I sent about four people to the hospital with broken fingers, arms and swollen face. Now I had to leave the neighborhood. The police were looking for me and the people I injured. Who were they? I did not know. It all started with Raymond throwing a rock. I had a friend drive me out of the Nine. I left the Bronx to my father's place in Manhattan.

Seeing My Father Again

I never knew where my father lived after he left us. I only remember he came to visit us once or twice. He took Richard and me to his apartment in Manhattan when we were still living in Willies Avenue. Years later, when we were living in the projects, he visited us twice. Still, there were no words of affection from him towards us. Not even an I miss you guys or it's good to see you again.

After those two times I did not see him anymore. I did not know anything about him. Until one day when I was around seventeen. My mother told me; her sister Elizabeth told her my father lived in her neighborhood. Elizabeth told my mother exactly where my father was living.

So, one day my mom and I paid him a visit; I went because of curiosity. Once we got to his room, my mother left to visit her sister Elizabeth. I stayed at my father's place. It was a small, furnished room in a big building named The Midway Hotel on 100th Street and Broadway.

While I was in his place I looked around and thought his place would make a good hideout if I needed it someday. Later that day I met some of his friends. I wanted to know who he was

49

associated with. Everything seemed okay. When my mother came back and asked me if I was ready to leave. My father responded "He is staying." I guess he did not lose his style of demanding, instead of asking. He did not have an idea who it was he was letting back in his life. I thought it would be okay to get to know my father and try out the new hideout. I stayed for a few days, then went back to the Bronx. But I made it a habit to go back and forth from the Bronx to Manhattan to cool off.

After the night I attacked the people with the bat in front of I.S. 148. I knew I had to leave the Bronx. Those I injured could come back and shoot me. It was my neighborhood but that did not mean I couldn't get shot. I knew too many stories of people staying in their neighborhoods after they did something like I had done. They wanted to prove they were not scared. It's about a reputation in the streets, but they end up being murdered. Knowing these things, I always made it a habit to keep a low profile long enough to cool off.

My brother Richard was in basic training with the Army at the time all this took place. He left for Fort Silks, Oklahoma, a few months before. Now he was about to come back home. From my father's place in Manhattan, I sent him an overnight mail telling him not to step foot in the block. My brother and I looked so much alike. I knew he could easily be mistaken for me and I did not want to see him hurt because of me.

Now when he returned, he came to Manhattan. I explained everything that happened and we stayed in Manhattan for a few months. After a few months we started going back to the Bronx but not to stay. We would go late at night and look around, to seeing who was out there. I asked around if the cops were looking for me. It felt good to see the block again and find some home-boys who were always glad to see me and welcomed me back.

Chapter 5

BACK ON THE NINE

STEPHEN AND POP STAYED IN TOUCH WITH me; they knew where my father lived. They would stop by from time to time. One afternoon they came and got me. "Come on Gee, everything is cool back on the block. We missed you homeboy. We need you back." I was glad to hear them say those words. I needed to hear them. So, I got my things and we left.

My brother Richard was glad we were going back home and out of my father's place. He had not gotten the chance to go home yet because of me. Sneaking into the neighborhood at night from time to time was not doing it.

Returning to the Nine, I learned that some homeboys were either killed or locked up. Life was one of the brothers that got locked up. I was hurt to hear that news; I saw him as a brother. He was sentenced to three years to life. It had been his third felony. Three felonies in New York gets a person life.

Ernest Bolden was later killed in the month of November somewhere in Baltimore. The newspaper read *Bronx Thug Shot Dead in Baltimore*. Stephen, Chango, and I paid his mother a visit to show our respect. We then went to what was a closed-casket funeral. Kenny Harding had disappeared, I remembered he had told me once that he was planning on getting away from the block to cool off. Next time I would see Kenny was in a Riker's Island bus as we returning from court to Riker's Island. Although cuffed and separated by a cage we laughed and shared old war stories.

Chango Alvarez had being home for a few weeks now. He had finish doing approximately four years in prison. Now he was home and hanging out with Stephen and me. Chango, was as crazy as his younger brother Raymond. He was old school. He too, had been in and out of jail since he was young.

Being back on the block and idle, and having the accessibility to guns was a remedy for trouble. In no time we were doing stick ups here and there. Sometimes right in the neighborhood. Sometimes outside of our neighborhood. It became our means of income. Sometimes it was just us three. Other times we had other homeboys join us. It was becoming crazy, there was times we were not getting a tip on who to stick up. We were just sticking up people which we thought might have money. The worst robberies were the ones we did right on the Nine. This was our neighborhood. We were getting outsiders, but it was still our block. It was home. A main rule we had was you don't eat and crap in the same bowl. It was a rule we all violated one time or another but now we were over doing it.

Then I started noticing Stephen. Of all the prison war stories he had and for all the talking he did. His actions were weak. I saw him freeze up on more than one occasion. Then there was a robbery were Stephen wanted to commit unnecessary violence.

We had everything under control. We were about to leave and I hear the trigger of a .22 riffle click. When I looked, Stephen had pressed the trigger again pointing the riffle to the man's head. I stopped him. "Yo, man what are you doing? We got the money! Let's go!" Shootings against rivals was understood, but an unarmed man that gave us the money, I was not going to accept.

Sometimes when Pop and I were alone, we would bring up Stephen's war stories and laugh. This was because Stephen would have stories that didn't make any sense. And stories that we knew were made up. I guess I should have known better than walking with Stephen, but I continued to hang out with him.

The Last Armed Robbery

It was New Year's Eve. The trains and buses would be free in New York City this night. This was done to avoid drunk driving the news reporters announced. So, many of the homeboys agreed on going to Times Square for the New Year. I was with a friend we called Brains, and with Moses Louis, which was an outstanding boxer. We bought some bottles of Champaign; I drank with them. We had fun, we met people from different states. Things seemed different for some reason. Maybe it was because deep inside I wanted a change in my life.

The countdown started 10, 9, 8, 7, everyone pushed in closer to see the ball drop. I felt crushed, I couldn't breathe. Moses yell to me "don't worry Gee, this will last a few seconds." He was right after the ball dropped and the lights read **1985**, thirty second later the pressure in my chest was released. People started walking away, we could move again. The new year was here, I told myself things had to change for me this year. I couldn't go on living the way I was living.

The next morning, I started looking at the calendar to count the months before the summer came. I could not wait; the pool in Crotona Park was going to reopen that summer after being closed for a few years. I was thinking of all the young ladies that were going to be there and of all the swimming I would do. This was one of my hang-outs in my early teens. I planned to look for a job this summer, hang up my guns and just have stories to tell. That was it; I was not going to do any more armed robberies.

About a week later, a strong thought kept coming to me. Something kept telling me to take the shotgun and rifle that I had in my possession, but that belonged to a friend of Stephen. I kept thinking, "Take the forearms back to Stephen." It was like a voice in my head. I kept on asking myself, "What is going on? This isn't like me." It went on for some days. "Take the shotgun and rifle to Rodney's apartment if you don't find Stephen. Leave them there, Rodney will give them to Steven. Go to Manhattan, to your father's place." This went on again for a few days.

One morning I woke up and I yelled to my sister, telling her that I did not want to see anyone that day, "Janet, if anybody comes to see me today, whoever it is, tell them I am not in." I started to yell at my sister again, "Janet, if anybody comes to pick me up, tell them I'm not in." I guess she did not hear me because she yelled back, "Stephen is here looking for you."

55

Suddenly my room door opened and it was Stephen. "What's up Baby G? I got a sting for us to do." I asked him, "What? It's too early in the morning and you're talking about a robbery. We didn't plan anything, are you crazy?" Stephen said, "Nah, man, it's easy." I asked, "What sting; where is this robbery going to be?" He told me he was planning to stick up Maxi's pawnshop. It was about four or five blocks away from where I lived. I told him, "You are crazy. There isn't any money there." He insisted, "Yeah, man, they are moving. We could get them while they are coming out." I thought for a second and said to myself, "It is just a quick sting. I've done quick stings before." I told Steven "All right, I'll go if Chango goes." Deep inside, I was hoping Chango would say no. I was hoping he was not even around. But I looked out the window and the first crazy person I see is Chango, crossing the street. I called out to him from the window "Chango, come upstairs!" He signals me with his hand that he is coming up. I started out to take the elevator to meet him downstairs. We met in the elevator and I told him, "Stephen has a sting to do, but if you don't go, I'm not going." I was hoping he would say that he was not going. Instead, he immediately said, "Let's go. I am down, let's get paid." These guys weren't home not even a year yet. Chango probably was not home for six months yet.

We went upstairs and quickly started to plan the hit as if to do it and get it over with. We started mentioning positions, who was going in first, who was going to have what gun, rifle, or shotgun. Stephen even made his younger brother Vincent come with us on the robbery, knowing Vincent never did an armed robbery before.

Vincent would pick a pocket in midtown Manhattan but never had anything to do with a gun. Still, Stephen made him come but only as a lookout. When we were about to leave, I told the guys, "Wait, let me use the bathroom before we go." I went in the bathroom and prayed. Not out of fear, but out of conviction.

Some weeks before all this took place, a friend of the family named Miguel came to see me and shared with me some words he understood God had placed in his heart for me. "I have been praying for you," Miguel told me. "And the Lord has placed in my heart that your life is in great danger. Your days are ending because of the way you are living." When Miguel told me this, I believed him, but I did nothing. I kept living the same lifestyle I was living.

Yet, this day in the bathroom before leaving I prayed, "God, I know this is the day you told me through Miguel that I would die if I kept on living this lifestyle. I ask your mercy on me and I prefer to go to prison, even if it is a life sentence instead of being killed." I knew that alive, even if it was in prison, I would have hope. I was ready now and we left the apartment. We went downstairs and across the streets from my building, and we caught a cab, and a few blocks down we got out of the cab. I was carrying a duffle bag with a 12-gauge shotgun and a .30-30 rifle in it. Stephen had a .38 revolver. Chango was by me and he would use one of the two weapons I was carrying. Vinny was a lookout; he would just stand across the street.

Once in the area, I immediately noticed a man standing in front the pawnshop wearing a green army jacket. As soon as I saw him, I told Stephen, "This guy looks like a cop." Stephen said, "No, I don't think so G." Minutes later, we walked into the pawnshop. Chango went in first and I went in second. Vinny was across the street in his position. Stephen stood by the door to stop anyone from coming in. Chango started a conversation with the old man who was behind the counter, telling him we had something to sell.

At that moment, I pulled out the rifle with my left hand and then I pulled out the shotgun with my right hand. When I took the safety off the shotgun with my thumb, the shotgun went off. Boom! The shotgun blasted a big hole in the wooden floor. Something that never happened before. I then dropped the shotgun (which Chango picked up) and I pointed the rifle at the old man. I glanced at the door and the man with the green jacket was walking our way, but when he heard and saw the shotgun go off, he turned around and ran. Stephen ran right behind him. Vinny was screaming, "Let's go, let's go!"

I looked at the old man behind the counter (everything was happening so fast) and he was reaching his hand under the counter to press the alarm button I thought. He had a friendly smile, I thought to myself, "If he doesn't pull out a gun, let him hit the alarm. With all this noise, it's over anyway." He touched, as to press, and then pulled back his hand. I knew what he was doing and it was alright. It did not make any sense for me to shoot the old guy. Even in the middle of the robbery, I was tired of all the stickups and violence I had done.

Chango and I ran out of the pawnshop last. Stephen and Vinny had fled almost in the beginning, with the first shotgun blast. Chango and I ran straight down the street to Stephen's project building.

As we ran, we could hear the sirens. It seemed like they were everywhere. Then I heard, "Freeze. Police!" and immediately a shot was fired at me. I thought to myself, "If I keep on running, he will kill me with the next shot." I turned around and fired back with the .30-30 rifle I still had in my hands as I ran. Chango, I remember, threw his shotgun towards an empty building and as I ran behind him, I did the same after firing. I threw the rifle to my left-hand side as hard as I could. All this took place in broad daylight. I saw people looking at us, eyes wide. A woman hugged close to her man with fear, putting her face deep in his neck. He held her tight. We ran and ran until we reached Stephen's project building and once in the building, we ran up to the thirteenth floor.

When I got to the thirteenth floor and knocked on Steven's apartment door, where he was living with his mother, Pop opened the door. I ran in and fell out on the couch. I could barely breathe. Stephen and Chango came in seconds later; they could barely breathe either. Within seconds, we could hear the police in the hallways and on the stairs, their radios playing, cops cursing. We were quiet and afraid. We stood in the apartment and peeked out the window from time to time. The streets were full of all types of police vehicles; everything seemed to be blue and white.

We stayed in the apartment for hours and when it got dark, Vinny said he needed a hit of cocaine. Pop told Vinny, "I'll go with you." So, they left. I knew it was still too soon. Stephen stood by the window peeking out. Minutes later he said, "They got them, they got them! They got Pop and Vinny!" I thought and hoped for a second that he was only playing. When Chango and I looked, they were cuffed and put into a black car. After a little while, I told Stephen and Chango, "Let's leave. They got what they wanted let's leave. Now is our break." Stephen said no, he wasn't leaving. Chango and I left. We walked down Park Avenue and left the neighborhood. I told Chango, "Let's go to Manhattan, to my father's place." I kept thinking about Stephen, how he had stayed behind as if he wanted to be caught.

Chango and I were scared. It seemed as if every cop knew who we were and that we were on the run. But we made it to my father's place. Though my father could see something was wrong. Everything felt off. So, we left. I also thought about my brother Richard. We looked alike so much. I knew he could be confused for me. I did not want him to get shot by the cops because of me. Plus, he did not know anything about all that happened. I thought I should go home, warn him, and then leave.

I went back to the Bronx. Time seemed to fly by. Before we knew it, it was night again. At home, I met up with Chango again, because we had separated for a few hours. On this second night, I was in my apartment thinking maybe things were not so bad, just maybe the cops forgot about us. This night, my sister Janet was home with one of her girlfriends, Debbie. That night Debbie and I talked a whole lot. The night seemed so beautiful, just the way I would had wanted it to be when I was dreaming of changing my lifestyle. Debbie and I spent that night together. The moonlight shined in through my bedroom window. How I wished everything was alright so I could just stay with her for days on. Though my reality was a nightmare.

The next morning, after a beautiful night with Debbie, someone banged in my bedroom door. "Get up, get up!" It was Pop, "Man, am I glad to see you, how you get out?" Pop answered, "It is a long story, but they did not pick me out of the lineup … and I think Vinny is snitching." "What, Vinny is snitching?" It really was not a surprise. "Yeah." Pop continued, "And the worst thing is, they got Stephen too. I think he also might be snitching." "You think he might be snitching? What do you mean, you think he might be snitching?" Pop said, "G, in these cases you never know who's who." I told Pop, "Man, Stephen came home from doing seven and a half years; don't tell me he's a snitch." Pop answered, "I'm not saying he is but be ready for anything."

I left Debbie, but not before trying to tell her I really had to go, but I couldn't explain much. We were on the run again, this time it was Pop, Chango, and me. We left early in the morning, but we did not have any place to go. While on the run, a black car with tinted windows stopped in the middle of the street when they saw Pop and yelled out, "Pop, we are going to kill you Pop." We were not saved from the police nor were we saved from enemies. Pop and I pretended to be armed and we walked into the middle of the street, unzipped our jackets, put our hands in our jackets and yelled, "Come on, let's do this now!" The car tires skidded and they took off quickly.

Not having a place to go to, we ended up back in my building, but I did not go back to my apartment. This time I went to my neighbor's apartment, Denise. By this time, it was just Chango and me again. Pop left, it was too hot for him. Denise had two little boys, ages three and six. While in the apartment, Chango was in the last room watching television and I was moving from one room to another. I was anxious. Suddenly, someone knocked on the door very hard and Denise asked, "Who is it?" "It's the police, open up." Denise looked at me and said, "George, I have kids, I don't want any trouble." I told her calmly, "cool open up, I understand." She opened the door and they walked in, one officer asked me who I was. Another cop went in the back room where Chango was. I gave the cops a false name and told them I was only visiting Denise to help her with some housecleaning and the kids.

The cops were looking for George, the triggerman, based on the information they received from Stephen and Vincent. When the cops went into the back room, they put a gun in Chango's head and said, "Don't move, George." Chango pushed the gun away thinking it was me playing with him. "Stop playing G." Suddenly, about five other guns were aimed at Chango's head from different angles. He knew now it was real and not a game.

We were both then handcuffed by the officers. I was told I was not arrested, the officers just wanted to know who I was. But my sister Janet walked into the apartment and one of the older officers saw her and said, "Wait a minute, the twins." He then pointed at me and said, "I bet you're George." He then pointed at

Chango and said, "and he is Chango." They then escorted us out of the project building. The lobby was full of spectators watching the neighborhood thugs as the cops took us away.

That night, we were taken to different precincts for interrogation, lineup, fingerprinting, and mug shots. The fun and games had stopped. The situation we were in was serious. One of the detectives told me, "We know you attacked four people with a bat sending them to the hospital. You robbed a few guys at gun point, and you shot another man in a car." People are too afraid to talk. But now, we have you for an attempted murder of a cop. Let's see you get out of this one." I was surprise of how precise the officer was about each crime he said I did.

I was taken into an office and stripped. After I put my clothes back on, a detective sat back in his chair and asked me as if he were not interested, "Now, what's your story?" There were other detectives in the room. Very nervously I answered: "I don't know all my rights, but I know I have the right to remain silent. I have nothing to say to you guys." I was then put in a cell by myself.

The cops questioned Chango for quite a while. I could hear him telling them he was with his girlfriend whenever someone opened the door. I thought he was crazy because stories given to cops can be verified. After everything was over, one officer yelled to the other officer, "Keep those two together, they are brothers. They have a better story then we do." This was not said in front of us, it was to officers speaking down the hall from where we were and I overheard them. I expected and appreciated Chango's loyalty. He was old school.

Finally, we were sent to the bullpen of the Bronx Criminal Court where we waited to see the judge. The cells were full of other men also waiting to see the judge. The toilets were clogged up, with toilet paper and feces. The detainees were sleeping on the metal bench and all over the floor. One could barely walk without almost stepping on someone. To mention that the sandwich they fed us were terrible is to mention the obvious. Still all this was not the problem, I had been here before on prior arrests. The problem was the charges we were facing. I wanted to wish them away.

My emotions were crushed, I couldn't even fake a smile. I hoped the charges of attempt murder of a police officer, we were told back in the police precinct we were facing were just a scare tactic. The police were known for trying tricks as these to make people talk.

So, we thought that while in the bullpen, we should ask the court officers since these were different officers and they did not know what the cops in the precinct told us. I told Chango to ask the officer; Chango asked. The officer checked and informed us, "you guys are charged with attempt murder of a police officer."

Then, another officer came in and I asked him, "What are we being charged with?" The officer looked up our names in a chart he had and just simply said, "You guys have an attempted murder of a police officer." We were then told we were facing life in prison. If this was a scare tactic it was working.

After a few days in the bullpen, we saw the judge. The judge set bail for Chango at $20,000.00 and for me at $14,000.00.

After all the robberies we did, we did not have a dime. I looked back in the courtroom to see if someone I knew was there. I saw my friend Big George, who always gave me advice when I was on the streets. It was good to see a homeboy. I nodded my head at George, acknowledging him; then the judge sent us to Riker's Island.

It was what I always knew would happen someday—prison. The question was, when? I had been arrested before but after seeing the judge, I would always get a ROR which stands for release on your own recognizance. I signed an agreement stating I would stay out of trouble, and that I would return to court on a set date. This time, I was sent to Riker's Island. My plans for changing were over. It is almost impossible to take it easy in Riker's Island, especially if you are new.

Chapter 6

PRISON: AN EYE OPENER

CHANGO WAS SENT TO THE BRONX COUNTY Jail. I was sent to Riker's Island to the adolescence jail. I was not twenty-one years old yet, therefore legally I was a minor. It was a new experience to ride on the Riker's Island bus to jail instead of going back home as it normally happened when I was arrested in the past.

It was late by the time the bus arrived at Riker's Island. I was sent to Dorm 2 in the Four Building where the new arrivals lived. The next morning, I saw a lot of inmates waiting to use the phone. I did not think much of it. Yet, to the inmates, using the phone was a big deal. It seemed as if staying on the phone for a long time meant the inmate was tough. I thought it was ignorance. I also realized some inmates did not really have anyone to speak too. They would get on the phone, make their call and no one would pick up. Some, I realized in time, were holding a fake conversation. No one was on the other side of the call. Maybe they did this to show others that someone on the outside cared for them. Maybe they did it to prove they could stay on the phone if they had too. When my turn to use the phone came,

I used it too. Not using the phone would have been a mistake, it would send a message to the other inmates that you were scare to stand up for yourself.

After a few days in the Four Building, a Correctional Officer called out for inmates who were being transferred to another jail on Riker's Island, (Riker's Island has many jails). "If you here your name, stand up and make a line, you're moving!" I was one of the inmates sent in that transfer to C-73. This jail was also known as The Women's House because it housed female inmates, who were just as tough and violent as the men. The female inmates were not mixed with the men. All female and male inmates lived in separated cell blocks and separated dorms. Yet inmates, whether females or males, which went to school or worked in the kitchen, did interact with each other at the work-place or in the classrooms.

When I got to C-73, we were taken to different dorms and cell blocks for inmates to be dropped off in their respective areas. Dorms are open spaces which look like warehouses with lots of beds lined up in them. The cellblocks are long corridors, with cells on both sides facing each other. The cellblocks have a day-room which consists of an open space, with some small benches and a television. There is an officer's booth in the middle of the cellblocks. This divides cellblocks into two parts called A-side and B-side. I was dropped off in 2 Upper—the B-side of 2 Upper. The cellblock above us was called Two-Top. Inmates from 2 Upper could not see inmates from 2 Top. Those inmates were on a different floor above us.

Each house or dorm had its own reputation for being violent or soft. Soft meant the house was weak. Inmates called 2 Upper the House of Suffer. Two Top was known as the Butcher Shop, because anyone there could be sliced, meaning cut with a razor, for the slightest thing. Although, in reality, an inmate can be sliced in any jail for the most insignificant reason.

Being incarcerated was a quick eye-opener for me in some ways. I saw so many petty things right from the very beginning. The fights over the phone, inmates having to vote by a show of hands to watch a television program. At times an inmate would damage the television by throwing a cup of water in the back of the TV if his group lost the vote. So, the other inmates that won the vote could not watch their program. In fact, that cell block would not have a TV for days or weeks.

I quickly realize I was watching young men acting like little kids. But I couldn't do anything about it. I was already inside, I was locked up myself, and I too was young. So, I just went along with the program. My first fight took place over the TV. Siting down in the dayroom and watching TV in my new home. An inmate sat right in front of me. I said excuse me, but he did not move a bit. I understood he did not hear me so I said excuse me a few times. After that I yelled at him. "Yo, homeboy what's up man, you don't hear?" All of a sudden, all the inmates present got up and turned to me yelling at me. "What's up, you want beef, why you reefing?" Immediately I realize this was some kind of set up to start trouble with me or just jump me. I thought quick, "don't show fear and don't back down." So, I yelled back. "what, yall wanna fight, I'll fight all of you, one on one." The inmate that sat in front of me, which basically started the whole incident said "you want to fight?" When I yelled back "yeah." He pointed at another inmate and said "fight him." I thought to myself "this dude is a punk." The other inmate and I spoke to the correctional officer asking him to let us fight. After the C.O. asked us if we were both up to fighting clean with no knife, and we answered yes. He told us, "you guys have three minutes, that's it." Then he allowed us into a room and we slugged it out. It was a matter of fighting win or lose and never backing down. I felt good, I stood up for myself, as a man should. About two days later while coming back from the last chow (as dinner is called) of the day. I was approached by a pretty big muscular inmate. "Yo, homeboy you the one that fought the other day with my homeboy?" Yeah, that's me." Before I knew it, I was jumped by more than one inmate. Punches and elbows from different sides. The C.O. on the shift jumped in and broke it up. He was furious, "back up everyone, back up!" After the C.O. calm things down, he asked me. "who did this, what happened?" I looked at him and said "who did what?" "I'm not a snitch, I don't have nothing to say."

Little did I know that behind the screen door the head inmate that ran the house was watching. "Pss, pss, shorty, shorty over here. Don't worry man all new inmate get initiated. It's not a choice. You did good, this way we know who stands up for themselves, who is a snitch and who is not. You did good, you could live here. No one is going to mess with you anymore."

My fight over the television, was really about respect. I thought I did good because you can't let anything slide. This was not the streets. Where you could walk away, maybe. And this was not a movie neither. It did not happen like I thought where you fight and you're in. I had to be initiated, and not be a snitch. Now I was accepted, with time I became part of the house gang. I got my razor and some homeboys together—homeboys I met right in Riker's Island—Chino 13, Indio, Dwight, and me. Now I could get revenge I thought, but the truth about Riker's Island is that inmates are not sentence so the inmate population changes constantly. Some inmates go home, other go up north to the state prison if they are sentence to real prison time. Others are transfer to other jails right in Riker's. So, you live and learn and get over it. With time you initiate the new comers.

I started doing stick-ups in there like in the streets. The only difference is that in jail you use a razor or a shank. A shank is a prison made knife. My crew and I made friends with some kids from Brooklyn and made our crew stronger. We even had a white kid named John O'Connor, the only white inmate in C-73 back in 1985. We used to say he was the toughest white boy in the whole jail of C-73. He loved it. He would yell it out himself sometimes. "I'm the toughest white boy in all Riker's Island!"

Every day was a learning experience, every day you saw something new. The stories I heard in the streets were one thing but to be inside and live the experience was a whole new story in itself. Things did not always happen the way people told them in the streets, where the thug was always the tough guy.

I remember an incident that shocked me or probably just woke me up even more.

There were two young African American inmates that repeatedly bothered a white C.O. verbally abusing the officer, challenging him to take off his uniform and fight them. Telling him how they would beat him up in a fight if the officer dared to fight them. The C.O. was a very young-looking man, he was also skinny. To the inmates, he was a punk, a coward. They kept challenging the officer to a fight.

One day when we were all coming back from lunch, as we walked down the corridors. The officer, fed up with the verbal abuse, told the inmates, "You two guys are tough? Let's fight. I'm tired of all the talking you guys do all the time." The inmates answered, "You have the radio, and you could call for back up." The C.O. took off his radio and gave it to the other officer, who happened to be a young African American woman and the C.O. told her, "Do not call for back up."

I could not believe what I was seeing, I was always told that cops and correctional officers were suckers, cowards and only fought in groups. That they did not dare go one-on-one, head-on. That lie would be ripped out of my mind that day. The fight began right in front of all the inmates. Two young black inmates from Brooklyn and a skinny white C.O. fought and the officer beat the two inmates down. They quit on him; they literally ran into the cellblock area. Both of the inmates ran, it was incredible.

Scales fell off my eyes that day, how foolish I had been to believe the lies I heard in the streets. I thought to myself, "First, my so-called gangster homeboy told on me; now, I saw a skinny white correctional officer fistfight and beat two black inmates." No one saw it as abuse from the officer. This is jail and they challenged the officer on a daily basis to fight either one of them, calling him a coward. The officer fought the both of them at the same time and beat them. Seeing these two-inmates act so tough with the officer all this time, but then see them run from him. The officer turned out to be tougher than they believed. This got me thinking about Stephen and all the nonsense he spoke. Always praising Capone and Luciano, based on movies he saw. I then remembered the times he froze up, during some armed robberies. There was even a time he talked himself out of a fight with the excuse that he was still on parole. How blind I was. He was all talk; that was it. He had no real action. I promised myself I would call things as I saw them from now. No more making excuses for no one, not even homeboys as I did with Stephen when I saw his fear in the past. If you can't take the heat, get out of the kitchen.

It was now August 4, and I became twenty-one years of age. I was, therefore, transferred to an adult jail, C-95, right on Riker's Island. C-95 was like a military camp, the correctional officers ran the jail. They were not accepting any nonsense from any inmates. This was not the adolescence jails.

One day, I saw something that also function as an eye opener to me, no matter how insignificant it might have seemed to others. Our block was in the mess hall; we were all sitting down eating. Suddenly, an inmate, about twenty-seven years of age, banged on top of the table with all his strength and screamed outload at the top of his lungs, "Damn, what am I doing here again? Prison is for suckers and losers." I sat there and waited to see if someone would say, "Yo brother, you are disrespecting me. I'm not a loser or a sucker."

I wanted to see who would step up to him, because I believe his statement had to offend somebody. But nobody said nothing, not a word. I laughed inside and thought, "He is probably right, this is for suckers and loser." I realized that I had to survive and go home one day, never to come back.

During tensions and rumors of a riot, I remember over hearing a captain telling his officers, as the inmates worked out in the yard, "If the riot breaks out, put your backs to the fence and leave. We can't stop them; we will come in after everything is over." I was in the yard that day, working out and looking forward to the riot that never happened. Inmates were then transferred to different jails because of the possible riot. I was sent to another jail: North Facility.

North Facility was a new building that had no cells, only dorms. It was clean and had a nice, big yard. In my mind, I always compared it with a federal prison even though I had never been in one. At North Facility, I ran into some brothers I knew from the streets and was disappointed. One had temporarily lost his mind and would hide behind chairs he himself stacked up, one on top of the other. Then, he would read the bible and peak out from behind the chairs. Others were just simply scared to fight or get stabbed as they themselves expressed to me when I asked them what was happening with them. Another claimed to be a pimp but did not have a dollar to bail himself out when the courts gave him a dollar bail.

This was plainly disappointing. What did I get myself into? I saw old inmates bragging that this arrest was not their first time, but their third time. As if it were a trophy or a college degree. Still, others would brag saying, "I am not new to this, I am true to this." Some would even tell younger inmates "If you change, you were never real." I would sarcastically ask, "Real to what?"

It came to the point where I just wanted to get my case over with. Go do my time in the state prison and eventually go home. Going back and forth to court is known among inmates as bullpen therapy. It drains a person; it makes an inmate want to take a plea deal and leave up north. As the state prison are called. This can work even on a person who has been falsely accused. In my case, I knew I was not innocent. So, I was ready to take a plea bargain.

After fourteen months in Riker's Island, the courts went from offering me fifteen to life to offering me eight years and four months to twenty-five years. This deal meant I had to do seven more years before I would see the parole board. I took the plea. My co-defendants Stephen, told on me and Chango had already taken a plea.

I had told Chango, "If they offer you a plea with just a few years, take it." He told me "No, I am not doing that to you." I told him, "Don't be stupid; these guys told on us already. If they offer you a plea, take it." Chango did not want to take a plea because an inmate has to say everything that happened on the day of the crime in order to take the plea deal—in other words, confess.

74

"Yes, I was there and so was George." But we held strong from the beginning and we never told on each other. I did not want him to go to trial, lose the case, and end up getting more time. I told him again, "I am giving you permission, take a plea." I later learned they offered him four to eight years, and I was glad he took it.

Sent Up North

After I took the plea deal, I was sent to House of Detention for Men, better known as H.D.M. I was there for two weeks then it was time to go up north, to the big house. My first trip was Downstate Correctional Facility, which is a reception prison for adults where you first get your inmate number. This number becomes your new name from that time on. Your hair is cut down bald and your face is cleanly shaved. Last your given a green uniform that becomes your main outfit while in prison.

While in Downstate, I saw Pop again. Last time I saw him was when Chango and I were on the run. Pop, had informed me that Stephen might be snitching. I did not believe him back then, but now I knew it was true.

It was a good thing to see Pop again. We talked a lot every chance we got. I was starting to see the state prisons weren't like Riker's Island. Up here inmates had to lock in by 4:00 p.m. and we came out just to eat. We walked to the mess hall ate and then it was back to the unit and in to our individual cells. When we were let out of our cells for recreation, it was for an hour in a dayroom. There we talked and planned. We agreed that armed robberies were over. So, we promised we would become contract killers. Whoever wanted someone dead, all they had to do was call us and we would take care of it and the person would pay us. We were thinking crazy. Pop was already sentenced to seven years to life for the murder he had committed. Yet, this would be the last time I saw Pop. He was transferred to another prison.

While in Downstate C. F. I saw a counselor as all inmates do. This is the purpose of the reception prison of Downstate, for inmates to be evaluated by the state as in medical conditions. Nature of their crime, work plan while in incarcerated and so on.

The counselor asked me if I had any enemies in any of the state prisons. This question is important because many times inmates do have enemies from the streets. Or inmates have made enemies while in Riker's Island. Whether these enemies are gang related or a victim an inmate hurt when he was in the streets. The victim could have a relative in prison that wants revenge.

I told the counselor I had no enemies. She asked me, "Are you sure? Because I have a Stephen Harris, who reported to his counselor that you want to kill him." I was surprised to hear her say that. After a few seconds of me thinking about the information Stephen had given. I told my counselor, "All right, keep it as he said." This was a wise choice I made. To avoid running in to him and ruining my time. I would wait to see him in the streets, I told myself.

Now where ever Stephen was, I was not allowed to be. The word I received was that Stephen was in Attica. This prison is way up in Buffalo New York. I lease I knew, I would not be transfer way up there.

When I left Downstate, I was transfer to Great Meadow Correctional Facility. Better known as Comstock. Comstock was a prison many called the Gladiator School. All the inmates which arrived at Comstock in our transfer were sent to D-block, which at the time was a reception block. We were only allowed to have recreation in D-block and go out to the D-block yard. Then back to the cells. We were not allowed into the general population.

This could have been because of overcrowding in the state prisons. We even ate on D-block. The block had tables and the meals would be brought into our block—breakfast, lunch, and dinner. There were three televisions right on the block and they all played the same VHS movies.

Mr. Parttee

Cells are next to each other in a long corridor. Depending on how many cells that cell block holds, they can go from one to fifty easy. Inmates therefore rely on one another when in their cells to pass things to each other. Being that we were already in our cells, the inmate next door called out to me. "What's up young-ster, can you pass this down to the guy in the next cell?" "Give it here old man." "My name is Mr. Parttee, what's yours?" "My homeboys call me G." That's how Mr. Parttee and I met. He was an old-timer, maybe in his mid-to late-forties.

Here I ran into some homeboys I knew from the adolescence in Riker's Island. So, we formed our crew again. Many of the old-timers, including Mr. Parttee, having been in prison before; knew befriending the young inmates was one way to stay safe. Or totally staying away from the young wilder inmates.

Mr. Parttee and I hit it off well and in time he asked me what I was in for. Then he asked the famous question everyone asks in prison: "Are you guilty or were you wrongfully convicted?" I laughed and told him I was guilty. "Youngster, you are the only guilty one in here." "Then I will be the only one that's guilty but there is no use in lying to myself." I then told Mr. Parttee that I was guilty, but that the courts were not fair with me. Then he was the one laughing. "What's up Mr. Parttee, what you laughing at?" "Well, youngster you think you were fair when you held a gun to some person's face and took their hard-earned money? Now you are looking for the courts to be fair with you? Come on, man." I had to laugh and tell him, "I guess you are right."

Being Mr. Parttee's neighbor turned out being a blessing. He made me think. Whenever I said something that was out of hand, Mr. Parttee would turn it into a question and reverse it back at me. I could not complain to Mr. Parttee; he would just say something that would have me thinking about the topics, organizing my thoughts and conversation.

Clinton Dannemora

Eventually, from Comstock, we were transferred to Clinton Dannemora Correctional Facility. Way up in Dannemora, New York. I had heard about Clinton Dannemora C.F. from other inmates when I was still in Riker's Island. Inmates told me how violent this prison was, but I did not understand until I got there and it was violent. It seemed as if there was a stabbing every day or some type of violent confrontation. I even got to see an inmate hit another inmate over the head with a big rock he found in the yard. When the inmate fell to the floor shaking as he tried to get up and other inmates were going to help the injured inmate, they were warned by other inmates not to help him. "Don't touch him, don't touch him. The C. O. will blame you for the incident." Immediately, the inmate was left alone on the floor as everyone turned away from him.

Clinton C. F. is located so far up in New York State that it is near Canada. The winter seemed to last ten months. It was so cold that I got to see an inmate with a mental health condition cry like a little child as he tried to zip up his jacket. His fingers curled up from the cold.

The first thing I did when I got to Clinton C. F. was called my mother and tell her not to visit me because of the distance. This prison was a man-made hell. If you had any bit of compassion in you, any bit of love, you really had to hold on to it, because it would eventually disappear as fog eventually disappears.

The mess hall was segregated. Blacks would sit on the right-hand side and the whites and Latinos would sit on the left-hand side. I remember the first time I walked into the mess hall and this was explained to me by a young Cuban friend, Jose. I told him, "You have to be kidding me?" He said, "No man, that's the way it is." I was shocked and offended. I told Jose, "Man, if it's like this, I have to sit on the right-hand side." Jose asked me why. I explained to Jose I grew up in a predominantly African-American neighborhood. "I am not coming to prison to act like this."

It was not the first time I found myself telling other inmates I grew up in a predominantly African American neighborhood. In Riker's Island North Facility jail, I found myself defending Bold, an African American inmate. He was from Harlem New York. He had knocked out a Puerto Rican inmate. The other Puerto Ricans in the dorm wanted to jump Bold, but Bold and I had become very good friends. Plus, I saw the Puerto Rican start the fight. It literally almost turned in to a racial riot and I was with the blacks. Some of whom I knew from the streets. Now here in Clinton's mess hall inmates were segregated. I went and sat on the right-hand side for the next six months while in Clinton C.F.

Clinton C. F. has an annex which is a Max B. All inmates knew about Clinton Annex. Many inmates wanted to get transferred to the annex. I was one of them, but I did not know how to go about it. One day, Lenny, an Italian-American inmate I met in Comstock, told me he was being transferred to the annex. I asked how this happened. "I wrote a letter to the administration and told them I wanted a transfer. You should try it. The most they could say is no." I thought it was a good idea, so I wrote a short letter asking to be transferred. Two weeks later, they gave me the OK for the transfer and a month later I was in the annex.

Chapter 7

THE ANNEX AND THE LIST

THE ANNEX HAD NO CELLS, INMATES LIVED in dorms. Each dorm had a dayroom with a television and a kitchen with a refrigerator, stove and oven. This was a piece of freedom. Inmates in a regular max prison use their toilets as a refrigerator. And cook in hotpots, which is a small electric pot that has an extension cord for plugging into the wall. This will cause the hotpot to heat up and cook the food that was put in it.

Yet ironically, it was in the annex where I had more space and freedom. That I would have an experience that I interpreted as claustrophobia. One night, as I laid in my bed the reality of my time hit me. "I was given a max of twenty-five years to do, with a minimum of eight years and four months." "I only have two years in, I still have six more years to go." I started remembering all the times people would give me advice in the streets. "Baby G, take it easy, you are going to get killed or go to prison." I remembered all the times Moses the boxer told me to take it easy. This was a man who did time himself. As I lay there remembering everyone's advice, their voices came alive in my head. I could hear their mumbling, "Stay out of trouble 'G' you are going to get killed; you are going to prison." "They are going to kill you!" "You're going to prison!" I jumped up and sat on my bed. "What's happening?" I shook my head and got out of bed. "What is going on, am I going crazy?" I couldn't fall asleep. I walked around the dorm for a little while and spoke with other inmates who were awoke. I told no one what I had just experienced. When I felt better, I went to bed. The next morning, I could not believe the experience I had the night before.

To distinguish the prison of Clinton Dannemora, from Clinton Annex, we called Clinton Dannemora THE WALL, for the big wall that surrounded the whole prison. The annex was actually surrounded by three fences, mountains, and nature. Although the annex had fences and no walls, if an inmate was to escape, he would still be caught. The prison was way up in the mountains.

One day in a conversation with other inmates, I mentioned an inmate named Ike, a friend. "Little Ike must be home right now, chilling." "Which little Ike—skinny Ike that was missing part of his ear?" Ike had gotten the top of his ear bitten off in a fight. "Yeah, that Ike." I said. "Ike is dead, man." The inmate informed me. "You crazy, Ike and I were talking two months ago when I was still in the Wall." I continued, "We were speaking as we worked out." The inmate again assured me Ike was dead. "Yo, 'G' Ike went home and was shot in the back after robbing a store with some homeboy. He is dead man."

I thought to myself, "Ike never told me he was that short to go home." I felt a dark cloud come over me, I turned into that little kid who left the elementary school that day at 3:00 o'clock and saw the dead body of a man who was carrying his little daughter. Ike was gone forever. All I could remember was the last time I saw Ike. It was a sunny day with a beautiful light blue sky and we were working out in the yard, laughing and having a prison yard conversation.

I knew I could not continue living this type of life when I go home. I thought to myself, "I am not going to be coming back to prison. I cannot be like one of those old inmates I saw in Riker's Island. Bragging because they had been to prison on numerous occasions." I also remembered the inmate in C-95 who yelled out, "Prison is for losers!" I thought, "I am not going to be one of them."

Reflecting on change, I started to think on the programs that different prisons offered. I thought to myself, "I will make a list of the programs I know exist for inmates." Ever since I was very young, I had the habit of writing things down. I did this to remind myself of what to do during the day. Once I wrote things down, I felt better. I knew all I had to do was go to my list, look at what I wrote and follow it.

Programs take time to complete and time I had. Having programs completed would benefit me in my parole board hearing. Even though I had years to go, I started by putting down what I felt was more important on the list, but easy to achieve.

First, I started with:

1.Violence programs. (my case was a violent case, so I needed these programs)

2.Vocational programs. I wrote down all the vocational programs I could think of.

I continued my list of things, and finally, at the end of the list, I wrote down 'High School Diploma,' because I believed it was the hardest thing to achieve.

Though, I thought back on how as a kid I loved reading about animals, especially dogs. My mother had bought *The World Book Encyclopedias*. Whenever I had a question about animals or anything, I would look for the answer in those books.

Also, whenever my brother Danny had a question about any T.V. program he would ask me. He knew I would read and memorize the whole T.V. guide. Looking back and remembering these things, helped me realize I was not as dumb as my third-grade teacher made me feel. I just did not have the support I needed as a kid.

After doing my list, I hid it because I knew that whenever anyone wanted to do something positive in prison it was best to keep it quiet. Many did not have goals, and they would only try to discourage you.

The annex was like Riker's Island in a way. I knew inmates from different prisons, from back home, and I met knew homeboys that were just like I was, idle and looking for action. I met a New York Puerto Rican we called J. I. He was from the Lower East Side. I told him I had family in the L.E.S. and that I use to go out there to stay with them when I was a kid. J. I. and I became very good friends; he shared some of his life stories with me. He told me his mother was a Christian but his father had been a gangster and a cruel one at that. As a kid, he saw his father and some of his father's friends kill a man. His father, I guess to make him feel better, told J. I., "You saw that? It was like in the movies, right?" His father would end up tied to a chair, tortured, and killed.

I also met this white boy named Jimmy, from Long Island, crazy little guy. He was shorter than me, with long, blond hair and sunken eyes. We became good friends too. I liked Jimmy. He would run in the middle of the basketball courts when the Blacks were playing a game and yell out, "Hey, why there ain't no white boys playing in this game?" Sometime Jimmy would grab the basketball and hug it in the middle of the court. Funny enough, he would end up playing in that game or the next game that followed. Jimmy told me someone was writing a book about his case. The book would be titled *Say You Love Satan.* I asked him why that title. He laughed and told me because when he and his buddies killed the person, they made him say those words before they killed him. From there on, whenever I saw Jimmy, I would call him by the title of his book, and we would laugh.

After twenty months in Clinton C.F. counting the months I was in the Wall, and the months I did in the Annex. I was shipped closer to home. I left a lot of good friends in the Annex, but it was time to move on. I promised myself I would never see Clinton again. I told myself never to return to a prison I left. Returning would be going backwards. Go only forward until you go home, never to return again.

The greyhound buses that transferred inmates, the inmates called them boats. This boat was headed to Wallkill, New York. Wallkill was four hours away from New York City. Once I get there, I will call my family and let them know I am closer to the city.

Chapter 8

SHAWANGUNK

AFTER HOURS OF SITTING IN A GREYHOUND
we arrived at Shawangunk Correctional Facility. A Maxi Max
Prison, we were informed. Up to now, all the prisons I had been
in were max prisons. This one was a Maxi Max, whatever that
meant. "Prison is prison," I thought. Upon arriving, we were also
told that the prison was on lockdown.

A prison being on lockdown means there is no movement in
the prison for a few hours or even days. This can happen because
the correctional officers are doing a general search for weapons
and drugs. Or, whenever there is a stabbing in the yard, mess
hall, or anywhere in the prison. When that happens, the prison is
immediately declared under lockdown.

We later learned the reason for the lockdown was that an
inmate named Willie Vasquez had stabbed a correctional officer
in the chest a few times while in the visiting room. The officer
was critically wounded, but survived. Willie Vasquez would be
sentenced to life in the box behind this heinous act of violence.

Once the lockdown was over, I was sent to D-block. Normally,
I looked to see who I knew. In D-block I learned that our new

88

home, Shawangunk, was literally a square prison with doors everywhere, which were not opened unless an officer called and gave a code. Inmates were escorted everywhere. Each block had its own yard and its own mess hall. This was a way to control the inmate population. The prison had a main yard for all the inmates to visit, but that would only happen on weekends or when the administration decided. I was starting to understand what maxi max meant.

Shawangunk Correctional Facility had some of the worst inmates in all New York State prison system. Inmates with bad reputations were sent to B-block. B-block had two parts. B-1 and B-2. B-2 was for the worst inmates in Shawangunk. In B-2 they had inmates who had killed other inmates during their time in prison. Inmates which had killed police officers while in society. There was an inmate nicknamed Farmer, in B-2 who had killed other inmates throughout his time, on four separate occasions. He was never going home.

Now, beside all this bad, Shawangunk had its good too. For instance, each cell block had four individual showers in them. This meant an inmate would take a shower alone, with privacy, and was able to do so daily. In other prisons, inmates would take a shower once a week. With approximately fifty inmates taking a shower at the same time in the shower room. The water in Shawangunk was hot or cold and the inmate could adjust it.

The food was good. The cells were big and each cell block had its own dayroom with a television. At times, the inmates were given late nights. Which meant inmates were allowed to stay up late and outside of their cell. This happened with special sporting event, like the World Series or basketball finals. All inmates had to do, to enjoy these late-night privileges was stay out of trouble as a unit.

Yet, regardless of all these privileges inmates still complain: "Man you guys think all these late nights and televisions is something good?" "All the institution is doing is trying to make us soft; before you know it, this will be a prison with no violence." "That's right and we will be saying yes sir and no sir." I would hear them and laugh. I would think to myself "some people just aren't happy no matter what." I personally did not care. Shawangunk seemed like an interesting prison because of its modern structure. It reminded me of North Facility back at Riker's Island, which reminded me of a federal prison, although I had never been in one. Eventually, I was transferred to B-block after a few weeks in D-block. Once I got to B-block I was sent to B-1. B-1 share the small yard with B-2 inmates. The majority of B-2 inmates were never going home, they would die in prison. Still others had twenty-five to life and some hoped to go home someday.

In B-1, I would hear the inmates speak about the inmates in B-2 as legends. Describing in detail how one inmate from B-2, burned another inmate to death. This took place because the inmate snitch on him. B-2 also housed Herman Bell of the Black Panthers, accused of killing two police officers in 1971. Herman Bell always denied the charges and claimed he was innocent. I remembered as a kid having seen this movie. Two cops which were killed by the Black Panthers. Mr. Bell seemed like a smart man; he was a jogger. A quiet and sociable person, he coached basketball games.

Still, there were others who lived up to their violent reputation, like Farmer. Inmates called him Big Head Farmer when he wasn't around. He was tall, muscular and a good fighter. One day, as I banged some conga beats on top a wooden box that held weight equipment inside, Farmer saw me and came over. "Don't stop, don't stop," he said and then joined in. I was surprised. We were beating some conga sounds like Puerto Ricans use to do in the Bronx in the summertime. Then he spoke Spanish to me, which surprised me even more. From that time on, we played conga on that wooden box every now and then. We started working out together on the pull-up bar, which was the work out of choice for the majority of inmates. Farmer was a light-skinned Black man from Brooklyn who had just as much enemies as he did friends.

While in B-block I met a woman from Puerto Rico through my mother. This woman would speak to me about God and tell me she was praying for me. I believe this was one of the few people who evangelized to me effectively. She knew my mother, she learned that I was incarcerated, and told my mother she would like to minister to me. Of course, all this contact took place through the phone.

Getting Carl

Some of the C.O. in B-block did not like me and I knew I could not blame them. I was somewhat of a troublemaker and a wise guy. This went on so much that the head officer La-boy wanted to transfer me from B-block. While this tension was going on between the officers and me. Someone snitched on Farmer and he was sent to the box.

The box is prison within prison. In the box an inmate spends twenty-three hour-a-day locked in his cell. The cell door has no bars, it's a closed metal door with a small window. The cells in the box is separated from regular population. Inmates in the box are allowed one hour of recreation in an outdoor cage.

I was upset to hear Farmer was in the box because of a snitch. I made it my business to find out who snitched. I Kept my ears open to see what I would hear. Someone always says something. Then I heard that an inmate named Carl from A-block was the snitch. So, I set out to get him. Carl was a Black inmate who hanged out with the Puerto Rican inmates. It was a strong crew of good Puerto Ricans. I was known for hanging out with the Black inmates.

Knowing who snitched, I went back to my cell and made a blade out of a tuna can top. I was restricted to my cell in an administrative punishment called loss of recreation time. This meant I could not go to the gym or the yard for recreation. I noticed, though, that my cell door would open every time the inmates were called to go to the gym.

The officer was making the mistake of opening my cell. It would be perfect to hit Carl and get away with it. I could easily say I was not in the gym, because I had lost of recreation. One day, when the officer made the mistake of opening my cell again, I went out with the blade. I hid the blade in my waist and went to the gym. As I sat in the bleaches thinking how I could get Carl to go into the bathroom. This way I could cut him without witnesses.

Money Mario, an inmate I knew from Riker's Island came up to me; "Yo, Gee what's up? I heard this rat Carl is the snitch, man." I told him, "I know, I have my blade on me. I'm ready to hit him for being a snitch." Once Mario saw I was serious, he told me "I'm with you, like when we were in Riker's Island. For old time's sake."

We waited for Carl to go into the bathroom, but he never did. I told Mario to invite Carl to the bathroom. "Tell him you have weed." Mario approached Carl, but Carl said no. Inmates can feel the tension in prison when things are not right. Plus, the rumor was out that he had snitched.

Finally, the gym period was over and I told Mario I was going to get Carl even if it was in the corridors. Mario said, "He's a big guy and you are big too, why you don't grab him and I'll cut him." I told Mario "Cool, I'll cut him or grab him, don't make me no difference."

As we all walked into the corridor, Carl waited for some friends to come by. But everyone knew why he was getting hit so no one wanted anything to do with him. Carl mixed in among his friends, but I did not care. I walked up behind him and I jumped up, so high in the air I could see the top of his head and shoulders. As I came down, I put him in a headlock and he went out quick, unconscious. I bent down a little and Mario leaned over me from behind and cut Carl's face twice. I could hear the slice of the flesh. I then stood up straight and slammed Carl to the floor. His molars fell out his mouth, and his head bust open. He needed stitches on his face, mouth, and head.

Money Mario passed the blade to another inmate in the hallway and kept on moving. I kept walking and the officers who were nearby, seeing the commotion in the hall, moved in. We passed right by them. They caught no one, but everybody in the corridor that day was called in for questioning. No one said anything, not even Carl.

I was called into a room and threatened with new time. I was questioned for about half an hour. Finally, I was asked why I was out of my cell if I had loss of recreation. To that question I answered, "Ask your officer; he's the one that opened my cell and let me out." That was the end of the questioning. The authorities, steaming, sent me back to my cell. I laughed to myself as I notice their upset faces. It was their mistake. Eventually, head officer La-boy would get his way. By getting me out of his "B-block." I was then transferred to A-block.

A-block was completely a different world; in fact, each block was different. Inmates with different mentalities influenced each block. B-block had inmates that were never going home. Although there are lifers on every block. C-block had many adolescents, that also was a problem. D-block had many adults that were taking things easy, more relaxed. Then there was A-block.

A-block had many inmates from the Bronx and Brooklyn. The majority were young adults. Not old men nor teens. There were many Puerto Rican inmates, and many Black inmates. Karate Pete was on A-block. Karate Pete was from the Bronx. He had been president of the Ching-Galings, a gang well-known and feared. Pete was well-known and respected by many. I had heard a lot about Karate Pete ever since I was very young; it was good to meet him in person. We became very good friends. Jimmy Lee was also in A-block; serving a fifty-two-years-to-life sentence for killing at least four or five people in different armed robberies.

Throughout my whole prison time, I always hung out more with Black inmates. Many were homeboys I knew from the streets. Yet, many of the Black inmates in A-block, where from Brooklyn and that made a big difference. It was not about race; the borough issue was a stronger problem than race. Even though I knew good brothers from Brooklyn right in A-block.

It was here that I started hanging out more with Puerto Ricans. Everywhere else it might have been one or two Spanish home-boys whether Boricua, Cuban, Colombia, etc. However, here I made more Hispanic friends than anywhere else.

One day, while in the gym, Jimmy Lee approached me about the hit I did on Carl. He expressed to me that he doubted Carl was a snitch. I told Lee with the same respect with which he approached me, "What is done is done, but next time I want to hit someone you know, now that I know you, I'll ask you first."

Jimmy was very zealous about keeping the Puerto Rican unity. That is why he chose to speak to me about the situation with Carl, whom he considered a friend of his. Jimmy and I too became good friends.

Counselor's Advice

One day, I went to see my Guidance Counselor, Mr. Mannoia, on a routine visit. Inmates see their counselors approximately every six months for evaluation. Mr. Mannoia informed me about what programs I should take. He then emphasized the importance of getting my high school diploma. I had gone to school in Clinton C.F. but I did not finish. Didn't even care much about it back then. In the Annex, I worked in the kitchen.

Now, Mr. Mannoia told me I could not go to the parole board without a high school diploma. I could not believe what I was hearing. "What do you mean I have to get my high school diploma?" He then explained to me that it would not look good for me to go to the parole board after approximately eight and a half years and not bring them a simple high school diploma.

I was scared when he told me this, I saw it as being very difficult to reach. I thought if I don't get my diploma the parole board will keep me in prison. Deep inside, I knew what my counselor was saying was true. How could I go to the parole board without a high school diploma? I always thought it was good enough if I showed the board that I tried by staying in school.

Chapter 9

THE SHRINK

THERE CAME A TIME WHILE IN A-BLOCK THAT I was getting upset at every little thing. Maybe it had to do with the pressure of going back to school. Maybe it was the prison time. At times, I did not even want to speak to my homeboys. Even the big cells of Shawangunk seem to be shrinking. My thoughts seemed to bounce off the walls. Whenever the officers would open the cell doors late, I would lose my temper and curse the floor officer out from inside my cell and to his face once the cell doors were opened. I blamed the floor officer for the cell doors being opened late.

I would be so upset that I was only an inch away from making the mistake of punching the officer in the face. The officer never made a move or said a word; instead, he referred me to the psychologist, Dr. Edward Rudder. This was a good, professional move on behave of the officer. To remain quiet when someone is screaming in your face was considered a coward's move to an inmate. The officer did not seem to worry about anyone's opinion.

I would eventually meet Dr. E. Rudder—he was a young man who posed no threat. He introduced himself as Dr. Rudder and we chatted for a bit, he then asked me my name, and continued, "How do you feel about being in prison?" After conversating with Dr. Rudder for some time, he asked me if I wanted to be in his group. I told him yes. It was a program I could use in my favor, because of the violent nature of my case. The program would last approximately eight to twelve weeks. Of course, other inmates were involved. Some of the topics that were address were our incarceration, how we felt about being incarcerated. And what were our plans once we were release. Of course, these topics would lead into other conversations.

After the program was completed, Dr. Rudder shared some words with me alone. "George, you're not crazy, you're human. You're locked up, it gets frustrating. You want out. It is normal for you to get upset at times. You are a leader and not everybody has that; when you speak, other inmates immediately become quiet. They want to listen to you. You say a joke they laugh; you agree with something, they agree. You don't like something; they say they don't like it." He continued, "You could do something with your life, you could change."

Wow, it felt good to have someone understand me, even if it was for a second. I listened to what he said carefully, he made sense. But, at the same time struggling with the fact that I might be kidding myself. I was in prison and that was a reality. There was no hope for guys like us. Once you are in prison, your record is ruined. I only wanted this program and the high school diploma for the parole board.

Yet, I continue going to other programs Dr. Rudder asked me to be part of. Though at times, not even the programs appeared to be working. I was happy one day and upset the next. I would tell people around me I was never coming back to prison. In other days I would say "if a cop ever stops me again, I rather shoot it out until the cops killed me."

I then started reflecting on how I grew up and how hanging out with the wrong crowd got me in trouble. I could not really blame anyone for my actions; I chose to do what I did. Yet, in my troubled mind, I blamed my father for leaving me when I was a kid. I blamed my mother for being weak when raising us. I started to blame people in my mind for not being there for me as I grew up. I started to blame people for my mistakes in life.

Good Officers

When an inmate gets sick, he is taken to the clinic in the prison. But at times an inmate can be taken to the outside hospital. Due to my extreme workout routine, I experience an episode of what I acknowledge as anxious. My heart seemed to skip a beat. The prison doctor had me go to the hospital outside of the prison. At the hospital I was given a checkup and had an EKG done. All result came back fine and I was sent back to the prison. But I was given a follow-up visit. So, I did go back to the hospital a second time.

My experience of going to the hospital was an experience like the one in Riker's Island. When I saw the two inmates fight the C.O. It was an eye opener. The two officers that took me to the hospital were white. That made a difference in the neighborhood where I grew up. The only whites we saw on a regular basis growing up were the police officers or school teachers. Once school was over, the teachers left our neighborhood. That left us with the police and we saw them as the others.

The escort officers, had full uniform and wore their guns. To my surprise the officers were very professional and respectful. It was a bit confusing, what was happening? Weren't these guys the enemies? When I went out a second time, again the officers were polite and professional. They even offered me coffee and donuts. They made it clear. They told me they did not have to buy me the coffee and donut. But they were not going to eat in front of me and just have me watch.

This happened more than once. On another occasion, they asked me if I wanted to walk. So, they parked the van as far as possible from the hospital. They did it so I could walk on the outside and taste some freedom. I didn't even know where I was, but I enjoyed the walk. These same officers took me to my grandmother's funeral and the professionalism was always present.

Once I got back to the prison, I told some of the other inmates what happened. I told them how the officers treated me well and with respect. The response from the inmates to me was shocking. They told me, "Yeah, but that's because they are scared of you." When I heard them say this, it really bothered me. I was just sharing with the inmates an experience that boggled me. I snapped at them, "Scared of what? I am in handcuffs; they have guns and they could shoot me if I get stupid." I then walked away, tired of hearing the prison lies. Same lies I grew up hearing in the streets.

Chapter 10

SCHOOL

"YOU NEED TO GET YOUR HIGH SCHOOL diploma, don't go to the parole board without it." Counselor Mannoia's words kept on ringing in my head. I started telling myself I could do it. Whenever I spoke to other inmates, I would tell them the same thing. "I am going to get my high school diploma."

I then went to the program committee. The program committee recommended I go to school. "The program you have to take is school." I became offended and told them, "No! You don't tell me what I have to take." We went back and forth in the office for about ten minutes. After a while of the to and fro, the committee gave in. "Ok Mr. Marrero, you are an inmate and we cannot obligate you to go to school. So, what program do you want to take?" I then responded, "I want to go to school." There was silence in the office for a moment. Then, everyone just started laughing.

So, I was now in school and I took it seriously this time. I could not mess up like I had done in the past. I found out a homeboy named Chino was going to school too. We gave our word to each other that we were going to get our diploma. I kept a positive attitude and would continue to tell anybody and everybody I was going to graduate. I believed it too. I even got an idea that would help me study. I was going to get in enough trouble to lose my recreation time. This way I could not go to the gym, yard, or watch TV. I would only be allowed to go to the mess hall, my program. Which was my classes and back to my cell. Now, I could study.

So, I cursed out an officer and got my recreation time taken away for thirty days. I would see Chino in school and I would ask him how he was coming along. He told me he was nervous but studying.

Chino was tall and big, a young Puerto Rican. White, with blond hair. He was in for killing a drug dealer who was also the leader of a crew uptown in the Bronx. Chino had been beaten badly by this crew for selling drugs on their territory. They were going to kill him. They would spare his life only if Chino would sell drugs for them. Chino had no choice, so he agreed. Days later, once Chino recuperated from the beating, he received. The leader of the crew came to pick up his money from the drugs Chino sold. Chino tricked him. Chino called the guy into the building as if to pay him the money he had made selling drugs. When the leader of the crew walked in the building to get his money, Chino shot him dead.

Now here we were, trying to get our high school diploma. While in my cell I called an inmate. Which I heard was some type of teacher or tutor when he was in streets. I told him to help me with some tutoring on my studies. I was such a troublemaker I guess he preferred to be on my good side. He seemed to be more than glad to help me. He helped me out every moment possible. He would sit on the floor in front of my cell and tutor me. School was everything for me at this time, at least that was a promise I made to myself. I was not going to be a dropout anymore.

The day of taking the test was nearer. Then we heard there were going to be two tests. A pretest in which the student had to do well enough to take the real test. Chino and I passed the first test and we were very happy. The studying paid off. I just knew I would pass the second test. The test day came—this was the real test. There were a lot of students in the class. The teacher was giving us the speech before we started, "Do not be nervous, you guys studied. Take your time, but don't stay on one answer—if you have trouble with it move on and go back later". Suddenly, I heard voices in the hallway; the inmates were let out to recreation. They were walking and speaking loud in the hallways, as usual. I recognize Jimmy Lee's voice. He was not alone; the fellas were with him. Jimmy stopped and looked inside the classroom. I heard Jimmy saying in a sarcastic voice, "What's going on here, they are testing?" The fellas with him laughed and they continued walking. Suddenly, I heard Jimmy Lee from down the hall, still speaking loudly, say, "Hold up, that's crazy 'G' in there. What is he doing there?" They came back opened the door and said "Chino too. Fellas, come on. Don't waste your time; you guys are one of us, forget school. You two knuckleheads are not going to pass anyway." The fellas that were with Jimmy Lee laughed even louder.

To my surprise, Chino got up and said "Yo, 'G' he's right. Who are we kidding anyway? We can't do this." I told Chino, "Forget them dudes, we have been studying hard, man. Don't listen to them, we could do this." However, Chino walked out the door. "Chino don't listen to them, man! We could do this; we have worked hard." Still, Chino left. The teacher started the countdown to lock the door. "Whoever is not in on time will have to wait for the next test date." There were only minutes left to close the door, then only seconds were left, but just before she would lock the door it opened and Chino came back in. He looked at me across the classroom and said, "Yo, Gee, you're right. Might as well give it a try after all the studying we did." I was glad to see him return to the classroom; the test started. The door was finally locked.

Days later, the test scores came back. Chino passed the test, but I did not. However, I was not upset. I was glad for Chino and the teacher quickly inform me that my score was so high I did not have to take the pretest again. I would just take the main test again. I continued believing I would pass the test. I was not discouraged. Chino thanked me for motivating him and told me there was a time when he could not even read.

I continued studying and believing I would pass. Plus, the next test date was not far away. I studied and studied and the test date arrived. I took it and I thanked God because I found the test to be so easy. I just knew I passed. The test results came back;

the word was out that only two inmates passed. I believed I was one of those two people. Then someone told me they heard I was one of the two that passed. I walked into the classroom and the teacher was smiling at me. It seemed as if she could not wait to give me the news—I had passed. Out of so many, only two had passed and I was one of them. I felt important. I was not a high school dropout anymore. I passed.

The word spread throughout the prison, "Crazy 'G' passed the exam!" A friend named Wise congratulated me, "I'm proud of you. You said you were going to pass and you did. Even when you did not make it the first time, you did not quit." Wise continued, "Check this out (he laughed); all the fellas were talking about you last night on C-block, almost all night. They were saying, 'Yo, that crazy Puerto Rican G got his high school diploma.' They were telling each other, 'You know it must be easy if he passed it.' Another one yelled, 'I'm going to get mines too." I laughed and told Wise, "That's cool, but they better know I studied hard." We both laughed.

Meeting Junito

When inmates are transferred from one prison to another prison, everyone is on alert. New inmates, no matter where they come from, can mean new enemies. Normally, inmates in a prison know where the new arrivals are coming from. The word always spreads, whether it is by officers talking or inmates that have mail correspondence with other inmates. Transfers can come from Attica C.F. Comstock, Clinton, practically anywhere. In Shawangunk C.F. once the new inmates came in, the whole prison population was allowed in the big yard.

If enemies were spotted that could cause some type of conflict. A stabbing, also known as a hit, or fights would break out. However, even if enemies were not spotted trouble could still start. When new inmates arrived at a prison, they could easily be tested (to be test is to be put in a situation where you have to prove you are not a coward) by other inmates that were already establish in that prison. An inmate should never allow anyone to identify weakness in them.

How an inmate carries himself is very important, because it says a lot of about him. But to know if an inmate has been in prison for a while all you had to do was look on his inmate shirt. On the left shirt pocket inmates carry their prison number. The first two numbers are the year the inmate entered into the state prison. Add a year or two to that number and you will know more or less when he entered the city jail. Numbers can read as 87A0000 or 85B0000. If the year is 1990 and you see an inmate with a number that reads 77B0000 then you know that inmate has been out of society for a very long time.

In Shawangunk, once inmates came in from the big yard, they would lock into their cells for the count (officers count inmates making sure no one escaped, this is so in all prisons). Then it is chow time (dinner), then inmates would be released to the day-room or small yard. I would always choose the yard.

While in the small yard, among our crew was one of the inmates that arrived from the transfer. He was known by some of the fellas in our group. His name was Elliot, but everyone called him *Junito*. Junito had a 1984 number on his shirt—the present year was 1989. We knew he was not a new jack. Plus, he knew brothers from our crew. He carried himself well, one could see the confidence he had. Junito was in A-1, I was in A-2, but both sides shared the small yard. The next time out to the small yard, Junito and I spoke and got to know each other a little better. We learned we were both from the Bronx. He was from uptown, in 180 Street somewhere. Junito was doing a seventeen years to-life sentence for murder.

One evening Junito was hanging with his crew in the Bronx. They went to a club to have some fun and meet young ladies. In the club, there were other crews. Junito and his boys were having fun. Young ladies as anticipated started coming around. One of Junito's homeboys met a young lady and they started dancing. Suddenly, Junito's homeboy is approached by a jealous boyfriend. An argument starts, followed by a fistfight. Punches were thrown, both crews were start rumbling. Chairs are flying, knives are drawn. Suddenly, a knife is plunged into the jealous teens body. He falls to the grown, blood gushing from him. The rest of his crew runs out of the club. Junito and another homeboy of his pull out their guns and chase the fleeing young men. Shots are fired and heard all over the neighborhood. People were screaming and there was panic everywhere. When the smoke cleared, one of the running teens lay dead on the floor with a bullet wound in his chest. Junito was arrested for this murder.

Now, here we were in Shawangunk's yard, sharing our war stories with each other. Talking about past shootouts we had experienced in our lives. We became good friends. Junito express to me, "I knew we were going to get along when I first saw you." We then studied and worked in the same program. I had taken up and graduated from building maintenances. Now, I was taking custodial maintenance, and so was Junito.

I trusted Junito enough to tell him who I did not like and who I got along with. What I thought of the system, and what I thought of other brothers. I told him I was getting tired of all the jailhouse talk. All the fake rules inmates made up and then did not follow them. I continued, "Whoever doesn't follow these codes nothing ever happens to them anyway. If you can't make these people follow the laws of the government out in the streets, what makes you think they will follow some prison code in here? It is all a big lie." Junito laugh and told me I was crazy, but I believe I was making some sense to him.

A day came when Junito told me that he heard from other inmates that an enemy was here in Shawangunk. I asked, "Who, what's his name?" He said "A brother named Chino. He killed the main man from our crew." I asked, "You are talking about Big Chino? He has blond hair and white skin?" He answered, "Yeah, that's him, you know him?" "Yeah, we became good friends." I told him about the studying and how we manage to get our diplomas.

109

I told him, "I don't think your friend that was shot would have tried to avenge your death if Chino would have killed you. You would have been out of sight and out of mind." Junito said, "No man, we were all tight. We look out for each other." Still, I didn't agree and I let him know. "Everybody speaks of doing things for each other when things are all right. Yet, when trouble comes, it's a whole different story." I guess I made some sense to Junito again.

"I know Big Chino; he's a good dude. You should talk to him and forget what happened. Leave the street beef in the streets." By this time, Chino was not in A-block anymore. He was now in C-block. So, when all the blocks were released to the big yard, I presented Junito to Chino and they spoke, and made peace. Eventually, Chino was transferred to Green Haven Correctional Facility.

Junito and I never got into any real trouble together, but we promised each other that if we ever did, we would look out for one another. One day, Junito came to the yard and told me that an inmate had arrived from another prison which had gotten a relative of his in trouble in the visiting room. In the prison he was in before this one. The inmate was locking in A-1. On the side Junito was in. I told him, "Tell the guy everything is squashed, tell him you want to live in peace. Then bring him to the yard. We will take care of him then." Junito agree, "Cool," he promise he would do just that.

For the next few days, I did not see Junito. I asked for him and the guys told me he was confined to his cell. Days later I saw Junito, "What happened man, I thought you were going to wait for me?" "I was but I saw the guy in his cell with his face leaning on the bars and he laughed. I passed by his cell and I couldn't resist. I lost it and punched him in the face right through the bars." While Junito was confined to his cell, the other inmate went into Protective Custody. Also know as P.C. which inmate define as Punk City.

Chapter 11

VISITING THE CHAPEL

I STARTED TO VISIT THE CHAPEL ON THE Sunday services and whenever special services were given. Visiting the chapel made me feel peace within. This puzzled me, so I spoke to a friend named Johnny Ace about it. He said, "Yeah, it's normal that when you hear positive things you feel good." I told him, "No Ace, this is different; it's a peace within." I continued, "I can't explain it. It isn't something I feel better about because I heard something good. It's peace I feel inside."

Junito noticed I was going to the chapel on Sundays. One day, in the yard, he told me, "I see you be going to the services lately. I think that's cool, even though you are a thug, you go to the services." We laughed at the way that sounded. I then said, "It don't matter what we do, isn't God supposed to love us anyway, I don't think God gets upset if I go." I continued telling him, "My mom is a Christian and would take me to church when I was a kid." He was surprised to hear that and told me, "Word, mines too." So, I asked him, "Why don't you go with me one of these Sundays?" "Sure, I'll go one of these Sundays."

Although, I was visiting the chapel and felt peace when I went. Although, I invited Junito to go with me. I was still struggling with my own issues. I couldn't forget Stephen crossed me. He had snitched on me and I couldn't let that slide. I had to get him back someday. Even if I had to wait to go home for it to happened. I daydreamed about it. I also remembered some of my own relatives and wanted to go home and hurt them. I remembered all the favoritism my mom and aunt had with the oldest boys as if they couldn't do wrong.

One day, while on the phone talking to my mother we argued, because her husband (she married while I was in prison) complained to her whenever I call. When an inmate calls from prison, the person which receives the call must pay for the call. I told her, "When I was home and you met him, he didn't even dare look at me. Now he is a tough guy, you wait until I come home, I'm going to kill him too."

Once I got off the phone, I was so upset; I believe the other inmates could see it. They just stood out of my way. I went to a part in the small yard where no one was around. I did not want to be bothered. I was extremely angry. All I felt was hate. In my thoughts I said, "God, I hate, and I want to hate. I hate people, I hate..." and I started naming everyone I hated and expressing why I hated. I even said I hated myself. Finally, I said, "God, I just want to be understood."

In the meantime, in the prison, the word was being spread that a big special service was coming to the chapel with outside church visitors. The inmates were glad, everyone was talking about going, many expressing why. "Man, there's going to be women in the chapel on that day." Now, the word was being spread around the prison among the Christians who knew me and knew that I had been visiting the chapel, to invite me. "Yo, make sure 'G' goes; we have to get him there." Inmates were literally as excited as if it was a big concert in the outside world.

The day came for the big service. Inmates could not wait for the service to start. Six o'clock came, and finally, all inmates were let out of their cells. We were escorted to the chapel. It was very full. I had never seen so many inmates together at one time in the chapel. The guests led the service and they were singing. The preacher was a woman. She was very charismatic, and in between the praises and songs she would speak. It was not a routine service; it felt as if heaven came down to visit us that night. I could not believe my eyes when the inmates were standing and crying. The preacher was speaking and it felt as if the room was filled with a cloud. A cloud one could reach out and touch.

The preacher shouted, "If nobody loves you, God loves you! If nobody cares for you, God cares! If nobody is there for you, God is there for you!" Then, she turned and looked right at me and said, "If nobody understands you, God understands you!" I remembered my thoughts to God, a few days before this service. I could feel a knot in my throat as I held back my tears.

A homeboy from New York City was sitting next to me and saying jokes from time to time. I kept very still and avoided crying, but I turned to my friend and told him, "I don't play with God." He could see in my face I was as serious as when

I held a gun in an armed robbery. Immediately he stopped and said no more.

Finally, the service was over and we were all going back to our cells, but you could still feel what I understood to be the presence of God, so real in this place. The place, I thought, stopped being a prison for a few hours. The visitors were escorted out, the preacher was held by both arms as she was led out. Having been raised in a Pentecostal church, I understood the preacher was still under the anointing of the Holy Spirit. When I got back to my cell I reflected on the message and how the preacher looked at me and said, "God understand you!" But the next day came, and although the service the night before was one to remember, I was still battling with mixed feelings. And my present reality of being incarcerated.

Chapter 12

REALIZING I HAD TO MATURE

Snitches

IN THE FOLLOWING DAYS, THERE WERE A few situations that were troubling. These events would cause me to reflect on life. First, an officer in A-block started bringing in drugs for an inmate in our crew. She did this because she got romantically involved with him. This inmate would then sell the drugs in the prison. The same officer then started bringing drugs to another inmate. He belonged to a different crew. Eventually, someone got upset and snitched her out. One day, when she came in to work with drugs in her possession, she was searched and arrested.

We did some asking around, and kept our ears open. So, eventually we found out who the possible snitches were. We decided to burn their cells when they were in their programs. Burning an inmate's cell was a sign that they should be removed from the block. Some of the younger inmates from our crew came up to me, volunteering to be the one to burn the cells of the snitches. I had to choose wisely; I couldn't let just anyone make that move. I had to make sure that whoever I chose to burn the cell would not snitch if he got caught. So, I gave permission to a young inmate we called Colombia. The burning was done while the rest of us were out in the gym. Everything went as planned and no one was caught. The first snitch was moved to protective custody.

Once an inmate is burn out, that puts the administration on alert. Also, the truth is that in prison there are lots of people that tell. So, the officer that was on the floor with the inmate was told to watch our crew carefully. The officers suspect we would go after the other snitch too.

So, we sent inmates which the officers were not watching, to do the job. On this commission, Bronx and Brooklyn had to unite. The inmates which were going to do the burning, put towels on the floor. Laid on them, on their backs, and slide down the corridor floor up to the target's cell. Burned the cell and got out of there quick. In seconds, there was fire and smoke coming out of the cell. The officer seemed confused. We were all sitting down very near to him. We were also speaking loudly, so he could feel comfortable that we were in his sight. But, in no time the officer was yelling fire, and running to get the extinguisher to put out the fire. After some minutes of chaos and the officer trying to explain what happened, things went back to normal.

We could hear the officer explaining to the officers in the booth, "I was watching them; I was watching the ones you told me to watch. I don't know how they did it." We laughed as we heard the officer say he was there at all times, and he was, but we

117

planned well and got away with it. In fact, the officer technically was our witness that we did not set the fire.

La-Sun

One of the last violent moves I made was to stick up an inmate who had been a friend. His people held a meeting among themselves and gave me the green light to move on him. I let them know I was moving on him with or without their permission. That afternoon, I walked into La-sun's cell and I stuck him up with my shank (prison knife) in my hand. My homeboy held the cell door open so it would not close on me. This was done because the inmate had spread a rumor that we were going to hit him (meaning stab) for no reason that we knew of. So, I gave him a taste of what he feared.

War Stories, Reflecting and a change of mind

As time passed, I knew I had to change. So, I started cutting people off around me. I stopped participating in the violence that would take place. I did not want any part of it. Whenever someone approached me to tell me there was going to be a hit and that they needed someone to hold the knife after the stabbing or be a curtain (which meant block the officer's view). I would tell them, "I hope you find someone to volunteer, but don't count on me." I was getting tired; it just did not make sense to me anymore. Why were we doing all these things? I started to compare the people from the church I used to go to as a kid. I compared them with the people I was around now. I compared the two years when, as a teen, I decided to take church seriously. All the fun I had back then, the peace I felt, the good experiences I had. Over all, I thought to myself, back then I was free.

Jimmy Lee, at times would come out to the big yard as we sat around, he would say, "Fellas, let's tell each other some war stories. You guys tell me how many people you killed and I will tell you guys how many I killed." Other times, he would want to talk about the time he was in juvenile detention. After a while of hearing the same things, I started comparing my past to my present. I realized there were tough times in my life growing up, hard times, sad times, but there also were good times, times of peace, of joy, and even times of learning. One day, I told the fellas when they came to speak about juvenile homes and other violent experiences, "You know, we are not happy in this place, and it's because we are in prison. We all want out, but here we are, every-body wants to sit around every day and talk about the things that brought us here. Some want to talk about prison, others about the different crimes. Well, you know what? When I look at my past, I don't see prison—I see freedom, I see girlfriends, I see fun times." I continued, "I compared this life to what I had and I prefer what I had." And I walked away.

Tricking Junito into the Chapel

After a while, I told Junito "let people take care of their own problems. I'm not in anymore." I started realizing that many of the problems I got into, originally were someone else's problems. I decided, from now on, I will just stay to myself. The messages I was listening too in the chapel services, were helping me see that there is hope in life.

I invited Junito again to the chapel. He would tell me he was going, but never went. One day, I got the fellas together and told them, "I'm inviting Junito to the services and he tells me he is going, but then doesn't go." One of the fellas named Santos told me, "I noticed he always tells you in front of us he is going, but then doesn't go with you. This Sunday, we will say that we are all going, to convince him to go."

When Sunday came, the officers opened all the cells on both sides of A-block. Releasing all inmates for the chapel and the big yard at the same time. The chapel walls were made mostly of big windows; you could see the rest of the inmate population going towards the yard from inside the chapel. Santos and our crew walked into the chapel first, other inmates followed him including Junito. Once in the chapel, inmates started sitting down and so did Junito and me. The rest of the fellas slipped back out, including Santos. They never intentioned to stay in the service. Minutes later, Junito saw through the chapel window, Santos and the other homeboys walking towards the yard. Junito got up and yelled, "Hey, where is everybody going?" I grabbed him by the arm, and told him, "To the yard man, to the yard." He looked at me, "You knew it all along." I told him, "Yeah man, because you lied to me, telling me you were coming and never did. Sit down you're already here." He laughed and said, "You right." We stayed at the service and enjoyed it. It was, as always, something peaceful and different from what we lived every day. Chaplain Falú preached that Sunday. I did not understand everything, but it was about God's love and that was all that mattered.

During the following week, I could not fight anymore the feeling I had in my heart. Knowing that there was a different way from the way I was living. A way I knew was the right way, a way I knew since I was a kid. Now it was different, now I was an adult and responsible for my actions. Now, I understood enough to know I was wrong. I knew, nothing else I tried gave me peace, not the violence I once enjoyed, not the homeboys, not even the young ladies when in the streets.

Chapter 13

OFFICER BROOKS

I FIRST SAW OFFICER BROOKS WHEN I STILL locked in B-block. It was early in the morning, and he was visiting our block. We were all in the mess hall. An inmate point him out to me, "Look at that redneck; he is evil and thinks he is tough. He doesn't give inmates a break." He told me this as we walked to pick up our breakfast. By the time we got to the tables, my mind was poisoned by the inmate's words.

Inmates must fill in every seat when sitting in the mess hall; I skipped a seat on purpose. Officer Brooks called for my attention. At first, I ignored him but then I turned around in my seat and faced him, "What's up, what you want?" "You have to move up one seat," he told me. I then answered him, "I don't want to and I am not going to. Are you going to make me move?" Officer Brooks stood quiet and did not say anything else. After breakfast, all inmates return to their cells. Inmates were then released for recreation, my cell never opened. Officer Brooks wrote me an infraction ticket. In a day or two I would see the infraction committee. My punishment was fifteen days locked in my cell.

After I was transferred to A-block, I found out that Officer Brooks was in charge of that block. Personally, I did not care. What happened in B-block did not matter to me. Yet, I got to know officer Brooks a little better. He was more of a nice person than other inmates led me to think, when I first saw him. On a few occasions, he could have gotten me in trouble yet he chose to speak to me instead. One time, I was out of my cell when I was not supposed to be. I was sitting in the back of A-block, talking with another inmate who was in his cell. All of a sudden, I noticed someone standing next to me. When I looked up, it was Officer Brooks. I expected to be written up——an inmate being out of his cell can easily get in serious trouble. Instead, Officer Brooks asked me, "Ready to go back to your cell now?" I answered, "Yeah, alright," and went back in my cell. There was even a day that Officer Brooks surprised me. He called me over to the officer's booth, and thanked me for not starting any trouble in his block. I believed Officer Brooks; I believe he was sincere. He did not know I was giving the orders of some of the troubles that took place in his block. I learned—I had others do things while I kept a low profile. So, I appreciated him telling me that my conduct was good. He did not have to tell me that, but he did. He even thanked me for it. It was a learning experience that taught me not to judge by appearances.

Chapter 14

ACCEPTING CHRIST

ONE NIGHT, WHILE IN A-BLOCK, I WAS reflecting on my life and my current situation. Thinking about the messages I heard when in the chapel. Messages about God and his power to change our lives. I could not resist anymore, and I decided to accept Christ into my life. Why put off a message I believe?

I walked over to the officer's booth and called officer Brooks, who was working that shift. I said to him, "Mr. Brooks, let me in my cell." Officer Brooks was surprised "You, Marrero, you want to go in your cell, what's wrong? We get trouble out of you when it is time for the inmates to lock in. Now you want to go in on your own?" I told him, "No, everything is cool, I just want to go in if it's all right." He answered me, "Sure thing Marrero, no problem."

That night, I walked in my cell, I put a blanket up on the bars so I could have some privacy. I knelt by my bunk and prayed to God. I prayed the sinner's prayer as I knew it, "God, you sent Jesus to die for my sins, he died and you raised him from the dead. Wash my sin away with his blood and forgive me, I do not want to run anymore. Amen." I did a simple prayer as I knew it.

In that moment, I felt peace. It was as if my mind opened and I started looking at the things I did wrong and realizing I did not have anyone to blame but myself. I realized I had made some wrong choices in my life. I realized the way I grew up influence my decisions, but I made the choices. I could not go on blaming people for my mistakes. It felt good to take responsibility for my actions. That night I went to sleep in peace with God and with myself.

When the following Sunday service came, I went to the chapel and so did Junito. This time, we did not have to trick him into being there. He went on his own. The preacher who preached that afternoon was an ex-inmate. Reverend Falú knew him from another prison in which Falú worked before being a chaplain in Shawangunk C.F. Reverend Falú spoke of the change God had made in the preacher's life.

I enjoyed hearing the preacher, because he was soft-spoken and wise in the way he spoke. When the service was over, the preacher asked who wanted to accept Jesus Christ as their savior. I looked at Junito and said "Junito, go up and give the Lord your life." Junito looked at me and said, "The preacher can't do nothing for me God hasn't already done in my cell." I stopped cold when I heard him tell me those words. Then, I asked him with respect so he would not think I was trying to mock him. "You accepted Jesus as Lord and Savior in your cell?" Junito answered me, "Yeah man, I can't keep on living this crazy life."

I then told him, "I did too." Then, I thought to myself, "I have to respect what Junito did, I did the same thing." I was referring that each of us accepted Christ in the privacy of his cell.

Chapter 15

WALKING IN FAITH

DAYS LATER I WAS STILL THINKING ON THE way God works. It was interesting to me to know that I accepted the Lord in my cell one night and to later learned that Junito did the same thing in his cell. I like to believe that God, saved the two of us (that were headed to destruction) on the same night. The word then, quickly got out, especially among the homeboys, that Junito and 'G' were now Christians.

After this, there were times when we were in the gym and the fellas would yell out, "Praise the Lord!" Junito would say, "They are trying to be funny." I told Junito, "Don't worry, check this out." I yelled back "Praise Him, He is worthy!" The fellas quickly got quiet when I started worshiping together with them.

Jimmy Lee asked me once "What's up G, you were a gangster with us, you were a killer with us, and now all you want to do is talk about Jesus, Jesus, Jesus!" I knew he felt as if he lost two friends who were not doing what they once did. So, I understood him and I told Jim "Let that be a witness to you that God can change people." Junito would eventually have people call him by his real name, Elliot.

It was all a learning experience; we were new in the walk of faith. We were coming out of an old lifestyle to a new lifestyle. We were doing what we could and what we knew. We were not in the streets where we could have gone to a pastor for counseling or advice. I also notice Elliot was always happy, I would see him come out of his side of A-block smiling. When he would see me, he would tell me "A-brother, I feel a joy, man. I am happy brother." I questioned myself, "Why I was not feeling that joy?" So, I told myself, "It is not about feelings; it is about knowing God saved us." Though, I did notice a change in me, in my attitude. I became more respectful and calmer.

Inmates that were Christians before Elliot and I, also helped us by giving us a lot of support. They did not leave us alone for a minute. They made sure we were getting literature (Christian tracks and tapes). They did not have any Bibles to give us at the time, but they brought us different reading materials every day. I guess they did not want to lose us. I imagine they thought, "These two who once ran wild now are sitting in with the Christian group." That was a miracle. Elliot would read some of the tracks he got from them and I would read the other group of tracks. Then, we would switch them. This way we both read them all.

One evening, a brother told me he had a tape of Nicky Cruz and asked me if I wanted to listen to it. I said yes, thinking it would be his testimony, but he told me the title of the cassette tape was "Which Craft." I started to tell him to forget it but I thought it would not hurt to listen to it. So, I told him to bring me the cassette, so I could listen to it.

Once I had the tape, I played it in my cassette player. It was not Nicky Cruz testifying, it was Nicky Cruz preaching and he was quoting Bible verses. I was shocked and impressed; I told myself, "Wow, I did not know he could preach like this!" In fact, I did not know much about him except that he had been in a gang, and then became a Christian. I thought to myself after I heard him preach, "If this ex-gang member can preach like this maybe I could learn to preach too." An idea was born in me at that moment. I was going to study the Bible and become a preacher. Then when I am released from prison, I will go to a Bible institute.

Still, Elliot and I, besides trying to learn about the faith, had to remind each other of the new lifestyle we were now living. Whenever we saw either one of us was going to lose our cool over some situation, we would step in and remind one another to take things easy. This happened a few times.

One day, Elliot came out to the small yard with a big prison knife. I said, "Yo, man what's up with that? That's not the sword of the Spirit brother." Elliot told me he wanted to get rid of It, but he did not know how. I told him, "Just throw it away, we can't give it to the officers." Elliot told me if he throws it away someone might find it and kill someone with it. I told Elliot, "That's their problem." "No G, we can't think like that now, besides I promised the knife to Sha. I have to keep my word." I then told him, "Yeah Elliot, but what if Sha kills someone with it. Forget your word, throw it in the garbage, God will forgive you." "You are right G; I'll get rid of it." "Cool." Then he said again, "But what if someone finds it in the garbage and kills someone anyway." "Elliot, that is not your fault because your intentions were to get rid of it, but if you give it to Sha, trust me someone will get stabbed sooner or later." We were babies in the Lord trying to do the right thing.

In two other occasions I was going to get in fights and Elliot step in to calm me down. Elliot wanted to use the phone and it was a busy phone day, many guys wanted to use them. Elliot called next on the phone and just when his turn was coming up this guy, who did not dare get loud with either one of us before we were Christians, told Elliot "I'm next, I called next." Elliot answered, "No you didn't, I've been standing here for a while now and I call next before you got here." The inmate said, "Yeah, all I know is that I'm going next." Elliot told him "Go ahead man, I'm not beefing over a phone."

I could not believe what I was seeing or hearing. I told Elliot, "What's up with this punk; he wanted to beef over the phone." Elliot step in, "No G! We aren't moving like that anymore." I told Elliot, "But he wasn't tough like that before, Elliot, how he's going to get like that now?" "It doesn't matter G, we can't be arguing or fighting over little things no more. That's not what it is about anymore." "You are right, you are right" I answered, and we left it alone. It was surprising because I knew the old Junito had a temper not to be played with. Now he was walking in joy and letting people slide. This was a testimony to me of God's transforming power.

Still, another day, coming out the Sunday service, Elliot and I were walking around in the big yard. It was a beautiful, sunny day. As we walked the yard, I saw an inmate I knew from New York. He was one of the boys who was shot on the train by Bernard Getz back in 1984. We came up in the same neighborhood. He had recently come into Shawangunk. He was sitting down on the grass. When I saw him, I greeted him, "Hey, what's up man, I didn't see you in the chapel service today, what happened?" He told me, "Man, I'm not going there anymore." I asked him why not and he told me, "That preacher man, believes in speaking tongues."

We got into a small discussion over the topic of speaking in tongues. For me, coming up in a Pentecostal background, I was defending the speaking in tongues. (Later, I learned that the apostle Paul says, "arguments don't benefit the listener.") Yet, this was the beginning of my walk as a Christian and the beginning of working on changing an old lifestyle of violence and ignorance.

Elliot noticed I was getting upset. I was standing over the inmate, who was sitting on the grass. I started to squat down over him enough for my fist to reach his face. Elliot noticing my intentions and came running, "Yo G, what are you doing man?" Elliot grabbed me, "I see your intentions." I told him, "You see right. I was going to punch him in the face so hard he was going to start speaking in tongues right then and there." "Yeah, bro, but it doesn't work like that; it doesn't work like that anymore." Again, I had to tell him he was right. We kept on walking and spoke about what just happened for a few minutes as we went around the big yard. I went back to the block and called my mother and asked her to get me a Bible. I had called her before to let her know I had accepted Christ as Lord and Savior of my life. Now, I wanted a Bible. I needed to learn for real. Not just the rudimentary things I was taught when I did attend church as a kid and teen.

Chapter 16

MOVING ON

ONCE I HAD ACCEPTED CHRIST IN Shawangunk C.F. I was not there for long. A few months earlier, my guidance counselor Mr. Mannoia called me into his office to speak with me. He informed me I was due for a transfer. I was also reevaluated, and my classification was changed from max to medium. I was so short on the time I had left that I qualified for a medium-A prison. When he told me this, it sounded great. Then, he asked me, "Do you want a transfer?" I said yes, so he put in for my transfer and it eventually came through.

Yet, before I was transfer, I shared with some Christian inmates how their lives ministered to me, even before I became a Christian. Donny Wells was one of these Christians I spoke too. I did not know Donny before he was a Christian, but I heard about his reputation. He had been a thug once upon a time, but when I knew him, he was a humble Christian. Donny had given his life to Jesus and he changed for the better.

Once, while in B-block yard, an inmate stepped up to Donny over a situation. After Donny heard what the inmate had to say Donny apologizes for the misunderstanding and tried to walk away. The inmate, a young boxer with a quick temper, (Donny was a boxer too.) punched Donny in the face as Donny was walking away. Donny turned around and they fought like pit bulls in a corner away from the C. O.'s view. After a while, the fight was broken up and left at that. It was a clean fight between two men. When I first heard of this fight (because I was not in the yard when it took place), I thought to myself, "What is Donny going to do now?"

Donny locked in one of the front cells, on the first floor. I got up from where I was sitting and walked by his cell. Donny had a blanket on the bars, but one could still see in over the blanket (because inmates are not allowed to cover the front of the cell completely). So, I looked in over the blanket and to my surprise Donny was on his knees, on the side of his bed, praying. I was shocked and thought to myself, "That's what being a Christian is all about I guess, he has made a decision to be a Christian no matter what." One afternoon while in the gym, I approached Donny and I told him how his example to continue in the Christian walk after the fight had ministered to me. Donny smiled and thanked me for letting him know how a negative situation worked in ministering to me. I did not know it at the moment, but it was as if God was taking me to say bye to my friends and brothers in the Lord. I was getting ready to move on.

At the same time, some inmates had approached me and asked me about my change. It is not normal for people to change, especially overnight. A friend which asked me about my change, was a homeboy we knew as Vee. Vee, was a Brooklyn kid, and a good brother. I was passing by his cell one day and he called me, "Yo, 'G' come here man. What's up with you? You all right, man?" "Yeah, why you ask?" He told me "Me and the fellows are a little worried, you know." I asked him why they were worried, and he told me, "Because you changed man, you all quiet and things. You used to be wild. What happened man, (he repeated) we a little worried?" I laughed, "You could relax man, you my brother. If there was anything wrong, I let you know." I continued saying, "I accepted Christ as my Savior and I believe he changed me." Vee told me, "My brotha, if it's that then cool, but we were a little worried."

One day, while in the gym with Elliot and some other home-boys, an officer came up to me and told me I had to go back to A-block because I was being transfer. (Inmates are locked in their cells once they are called for transfer. This happens a day or two before one leaves; this is done for security reasons.) I went up to Elliot and told him the C.O. sent me back to my block, because I was being transfer. We exchanged contact information to stay in touch. Elliot told me, "Move on my brother you did your time." We said goodbye to each other and promised to stay in touch.

Once in A-block, I was locked in my cell until I left Shawangunk. During the time I was in my cell, I thought of some people who I had done wrong too that were still in A-block. I thought that as a Christian, I should not leave without asking for forgiveness. To those who were near me I had to ask their forgiveness before leaving.

I called La-Sun over when he was passing by my cell. At first, he jumped back when I called him. I told him, "Chill, La-Sun I am not going to do nothing to you. I'm locked in my cell." La-Sun then said, "What's up 'G', what you want?" "I want to apologize for robbing you before," I told him. His answer back, "I don't know 'G', you're too crazy." I told him, "I don't have to ask you for forgiveness unless I really want to. I am chilling now La-Sun, I changed." He told me, "I don't know 'G', you always say you want to change but then you always doing something crazy, hurting someone, or something." I continued, "This time is different. I accepted Jesus as my Savior." He answered, "Well, I guess you are leaving anyway 'G', so be cool my brother." We shook hands and said goodbye.

During the night, I prayed and told God I wanted to be in church, every day and that I wanted to learn more about his word. Then, I thought to myself, "Well, for God to fulfill this prayer, he would have to open the prison doors and let me to go home."

Chapter 17

SAILING CLOSER TO HOME

THE MORNING OF MY TRANSFER CAME, rumor had it that the bus was going to Sing-Sing Correctional Facility. I was glad because next to Sing-Sing, there is a medium-A facility called Tappan Correctional Facility. I was also glad because all this was next to New York City and I could smell home already.

We left for Sing-Sing and for some reason we got there very late at night. I was left in Sing-Sing and not in Tappan. "What happened?" I thought, "It must be a mistake." So, I just waited to see what was going to happen next. I was then sent to A block; I was told it was a reception block. It looked like a dump after having being in Shawangunk. I could tell it was a very old prison. The cell block I went to was very long. The cell doors were very small, and a few inches above the ground. An inmate had to lift his foot to walk in. Inside, the cell was very small (especially after living in Shawangunk's big cells). I could not believe it. I was classified for a medium-A, what was I doing here?

As an inmate who had years in prison, I just waited. I enjoyed the view because, to my surprise, the cell I was in had a window

(I did not know if all Sing-Sing cells had windows but mines did). I could actually look out a window. It was incredible. Freedom was right outside this window. You could see the water and the seagulls flying. Every morning, I would get up early, pray and thank God for his creation.

One day, I went to the state shop, and saw a friend named Hector who was working there. When he saw me, he was glad and asked me what block I was in. I told him I was only passing through because I was going to Tappan. When he heard that he informed me, "Yo, man, Carl is down there." When he told me this, I thought to myself, "It is as if you can't get away from trouble." Then, I told him, "I am a Christian now. I am going to leave that in God's hands." Hector was glad to hear I was now a Christian and told me he too had become a Christian.

I lived in Sing-Sing for about two weeks and got to see friends I knew from other prisons. They, knowing me for my past, when they saw me, would say, "Oh no, here comes trouble, Sing-Sing is in for it. Man, you are not going to last long here. You are going to do something crazy and get kicked out, way back up to the north mountains." Me not knowing a lot about the Bible then, I would just answer, "I am a Christian now. I accepted Jesus as Lord and Savior." They would laugh and tell me, "I'm not talking about Jesus, I'm talking about you. You are too crazy and Sing-Sing is a wild place. Trust me, I give you two weeks before you do something crazy and get kicked out; two weeks." After two weeks past, they would come back to tell me, "You know, I am shocked, but it seems like you really changed brother."

Eventually, I was sent to Tappan C. F. After so many years of being in maximum security prisons, I remember I went down (Tappan is right down the hill from Sing-Sing) with another inmate who came from a max prison too. We were both lost in how we should behave. I carried my bags (my property) and so did the other inmate. A correctional officer drove us in a van to Tappan from Sing-Sing. Once there, he left. We walked to the office where we were to report. We walked in and just stood there, waiting for someone to question us or give us an order.

Then an African American officer came out from the back office to the front desk and sat down. She said "Hi." She was big and tall; a strong looking woman who seemed like a veteran at her job. She was very kind, but showed a lot of confidence. We gave her our names and she told us what buildings we had been assigned too.

Tappan consisted of three buildings—building 9, 10, and 11. Each building had three floors. Once she told us where we belonged, we stood in front of her desk, waiting for an escort. She then asked, "What you boys still waiting for?" We asked her, "How do we get to our buildings?" She laughed and said, "This is Tappan, here you walk." I could tell she was not trying to be disrespectful. She was just giving us the message "You boys are not in a max anymore." Wow, to hear the words "You walk," was music to my ears. We left the office and walked to our buildings.

The buildings were close by, but to be able to walk to the buildings by ourselves was incredible. I could not believe it. We were walking down what appear to be a long street. There were the three buildings lined up one next to other. The street went all around the buildings and there was grass and even a tree. I could not believe my eyes; it was like a dream. I had not seen a tree up close in about six years. I went into the building and up to the third floor where I was assigned too. There were no cells, only dorms with individual cubes, dividing every bed. Every cube had its own shelves and privacy. It was also clean as a hospital.

Sadly, I immediately started meeting new jacks (new inmates in the prison system who did not know what a real prison was). One came up to my cube and asked me what prison I was coming from. My first intention was to slap him in the face for even asking me the question. Then I remind myself that I was a new person in Christ. I resisted the temptation and made some new friends. I even saw my old friend, Mr. Parttee. It was very good to see him again. I had too many years in prison for me not to know people everywhere.

One of the new inmates I met introduced me to other Christians in Tappan. David Gonzalez was one of those new inmates. David then introduce me to Carlos Torres. When dinner time came, I went to the mess hall with David and Carlos. David was one of the Bible teachers in the chapel and so was Carlos. We walked into the mess hall and immediately from a distance I notice Carl. The inmate Mario and I cut when in Shawangunk. He worked in the mess hall serving the food. I did not say anything to David or Carlos, but as we were getting closer, I thought, "What can I do now? He has a big serving spoon in his hand. I better act fast." I had my food tray in my hand, it was big. I thought to myself, "I will hold it with my left hand and swing it at him to throw him off and then I'll punch him in the face with my right hand. I don't care if I get kicked out." I had just gotten there and I knew a fight in the mess hall would get me kicked out.

Suddenly, I thought, "What am I thinking? I'm failing. I am a Christian; I can't think like this. I can't continue living a wild life. I have to trust God." I took a deep breath and walked. I put out my tray and Carl served me my food. I greeted him, kept on walking and sat with David and Carlos. When we finished, we left the mess hall. As I was walking around the mess hall building, Carl came out the back door of the kitchen. He called me and I stopped. David and Carlos, who I just met, kept walking back to the dorms. Carl said, "Yo 'G,' why you did what you did to me, I don't know." He continued, "but I don't want no problems." "What happened, happened and it's over. I have the scares and I'm going to leave it at that." I didn't know what to say. So, I just said, "Cool, Jimmy Lee and I spoke. If you don't want no beef then there is no beef. I've been chilling anyway." How does a person make peace with someone you hurt and had sent to the hospital? This was new to me.

Trails with a Purpose

Back in the dorm, David González took me around to meet other Christian brothers. Then he presented Jose Pérez to me, a Dominican brother. Then he told me, "Up in the chapel I will present other brothers in the faith to you." I asked what days did they have the services. I was told that in between the services and Bible classes, we would meet every day. On some days, even twice in a day. I then remembered my prayer back in Shawangunk, when I expressed, I wanted to go to church every day.

I finally got the Bible my mother sent me. It could not come in a better time. She had sent me a Spanish Bible because that was what I asked her for. I can't deny that at times I thought I was losing my mind. There were times I would question myself for trying to read in Spanish. The desire to learn how to speak Spanish better and read Spanish was something that came over me suddenly. I did not understand it.

I finally went to my first service and it was great, The C.Os. left the visitors with us in the chapel and left. The first service was on a Saturday morning, and in the afternoon, the inmates got together for Bible studies with the inmate pastor Ephraim Rivera. He was a wise person, set a good example of conduct and a great Bible teacher.

After the first Bible class, as we were headed back to Tappan, I notice some inmates talking bad about Pastor Ephraim. As a new Christian, it bothered me to ear them speak negative about the pastor. Was the information true? I did not join in to speak about the pastor; instead I went back to my dorm and prayed about it. "Lord, why don't you take this Ephraim fella out if he is all that bad as the rest say?" Then it dawns on me as if it was an answer, "What if he isn't the problem?" I changed my prayer, "Lord, let me see who Ephraim really is and let your will be in his life."

The next day Sunday, we met for Bible studies. Ephraim started the Bible class and I saw a friend, as if I knew him for years. I enjoyed the way he gave the class. I knew God was telling me something. From there on, I respected him and saw him as my pastor

As time went on, I was now closer to see the parole board. I only had two years to left. That also meant I qualified for work release. Work release is a program that allows inmates who have two years or less until the parole board to apply to work in free society. In this case, they would transfer an inmate to an institution in the Bronx, Manhattan, or Brooklyn, so inmates can work during the day and report back to the institution in the evening.

I applied, and it felt good just to be able to apply. Some weeks went by and my papers came back approved from the administration. I was so glad I could not believe it. I felt I had one foot in society already. Now, I had to wait for the papers to go up to Albany, New York, and get approved there.

Weeks went by and I finally received mail from Albany, New York. When the officer put the mail in my hand, my heart started pumping so hard it felt as if it would burst from my chest. It was as if I knew the answer even before I opened the envelope. When I opened the envelope, the answer from Albany read: "Denied." I was in shock again; I could not believe it. My world collapsed, my emotions, and everything fell to the floor. I was so destroyed for the next few months. I tried praying, but I couldn't. I tried reading the bible, but I could not even find the strength to stay seated.

I would walk the yard by myself complaining to God. I would tell him, "Come on, become human so we could fight." I was going crazy. It was so hard to feel that I was being played with, especially with something like one's freedom. I had been in prison for so long. If they had said no from the beginning it would have been easier. I would have thought, "Fine, I expected that," but for the administration to say yes and then Albany say no, it hurt so much. After some time, I accepted the fact that I was close to the parole board and that was going to take place in less than twenty months.

A few months later, David González applied for work release, and Jose Pérez went to see the parole board. I remember David started packing up his things even before he had an answer from Albany, New York.

He would say, "Faith without works is dead and I believe I am going home, so I'm packing up." I would smile and tell him, "Cool, David I really hope it works out for you." I really did; I did not want to see him go through what I went through because the administration had approved him too and he was just waiting on the answer from Albany.

In the meantime, Jose Pérez's papers had come back from the parole board with the good news that they granted him parole. Wow, it was good to see some brothers being blessed after so much struggle, I was happy for Jose.

A few weeks passed and while I was working in the mess hall serving food, David came in with a big smile. He said, "George, I was approved for work release, I was approved!" I was surprised;

"You are serious man, you aren't just jiving, are you?" He told me, "No way. I am really leaving." Wow, I really saw it as a miracle because David had the same time I had, an eight and one third to twenty-five years bid with six and a half years in and two more years to go to the parole board for a murder. "You really have been blessed my brother."

Chapter 18

WORKING IN THE CHAPEL

ON THE NEXT SERVICE DAY, WE WERE IN THE chapel early. Pastor Ephraim was cutting one of the inmate's hair (Ephraim was also a barber). He said to me, "David is going home and Jose too, that is good, but I am going to need someone to help me give Bible classes. Are you prepared, George?" I was very glad he asked me. "Sure, I'll help you give classes." Pastor Ephraim would allow us to give a class from time to time for about fifteen minutes to see how we would do and then he would point out to us our weakness and strengths. It was something that helped us grow in giving classes and in public speaking.

I thought to myself, "Many were blessed with their freedom. My blessing is to grow in the ministry." After David went on work release, I started working with Pastor Ephraim and I believed it was God's will. Ephraim told me, "I know I could count on you. Whenever I can't be around, you are in charge, you are my assistant pastor." It was good to see he trusted me enough to work with him. The ministry work was not easy work. Other inmates were watching. Once you started carrying a Bible and calling yourself a Christian, some would test Christians by asking trick questions.

They wanted to see what answers they would receive. At times some inmates would present attitudes they would not present before one became a Christian. I remember seeing it happened with Ephraim in the chapel sometimes, when Pastor Ephraim was teaching a class. I remember David would express his frustrations about it at sometimes.

I knew Ephraim and David were not afraid; these were inmates who were in prison for murder. They had also lived in prison for a time as unbelievers and held their own and were respected by other inmates. In prison, we knew who was who; a person's reputation travels with them. It's that one day they made a decision, a decision to follow Christ. Now, it was my turn to be in leadership, but I knew it would only help me grow in my walk with Christ. By working in the chapel, I had a different view of prison and inmates. I got to meet many inmates who came in looking for words of comfort and advice, which we gave to them through scripture.

The more I studied the Bible, the more I would tell myself that, "When I get home, I am going to a Bible institute." I shared my desire and ideas of studying with some inmates and only received negative feedback, but I would just walk away and leave them talking by themselves. I did not want to hear anything negative. I believed I could do it and that was it. If other people could reach goals in their lives, why couldn't I? The idea of studying became engraved in my mind, I was determined to study. I believed God would make a way.

Chapter 19

THE LOSS OF A LOVED ONE

ONE DAY, IN THE MONTH OF AUGUST OF 1992, as I sat in my cube area, reading and studying my Bible, the floor officer called me, "Marrero, come over to the officers' desk." I went over and asked, "What is it?" "You are wanted up in the chapel area." I got ready because an officer was coming to escort me up to Sing-Sing. As I was going up the hill, I wondered: "What is this all about?" I thought that I would probably be getting the good news that I was going home on work release.

I got up to the chapel area and walked up to the priest's office. I knocked on the door and his assistant answered the door. I told him who I was. He said, "Yes, we were waiting for you." My heart dropped, because being called by the priest, or any religious leader, only meant one thing—a death in the family.

I walked in and sat down, attentive to what he was about to say. For minute I was bewildered, I asked myself, "Who died in my family?" The priest started by saying "Your brother Richard..." and I thought, "No Lord, he doesn't serve you." The priest continued by saying, "...called this morning to inform us that your mother died last night." I was stunned, shocked, surprised, and cried for a minute, but maintained my calm. I asked if I could go down to see her at the funeral. The priest said yes, they were making the arrangements.

How could this have happened? I was just speaking with her Monday evening. She seemed well; now I was called to be informed that she had died around 3:00 a.m. Alone in the corridor, I cried as I waited for my escort back down to Tappan. When I got back down to Tappan C. F. and other inmates heard of my mother's death, they cried with me and showed me their respect. Jose Sánchez, a very close friend I had made in Tappan, felt deeply my mother's death, as if it were his mother.

Later that very day, I was called back to Sing-Sing to try on a suit and travel to the funeral home. I was escort to the Bronx to see my mother's body—the woman who saw me go to prison, but never saw me come home. Yet, I thanked God that she knew I had accepted Christ as my Lord and Savior. And on many visits, we spoke and made peace. I even asked her "Why did you show my siblings more love than you did to me?" Her answer to me was, "Because I always so you to be strong and independent. It was as if you didn't need help. Yet, Danny I saw as weak." Can't say I agreed with the philosophy, but it was good to hear her acknowledge that she could have done a better job.

I arrived at the funeral and saw many familiar faces from the church I used to visit as a kid. My mother had continue being a member there. I saw some relatives, uncle *Roberto*, my aunts and some cousins. I was asked to share some words and I did. My aunt *Teresa* came up to me afterward and expressed her gratitude for my words. *"Sentí la presencia de Dios mientras hablabas."* We spoke for a bit; other church members also came up to me and express their condolences. Uncle *Roberto* told me, "You lost a mother and I lost a little sister." My aunt *María* waited for me outside and we spoke some as I was getting back on the prison van to head back to Tappan C. F.

As we headed back, the officers drove me through my old neighborhood, the Nine. I just looked in silence, seeing how a lot had changed, but I never said a word. One of the officers asked me, "Don't you know any of these neighborhoods?" I answered, "Yeah, you just drove me through my old neighborhood." He then asked, "Why didn't you say anything?" I told him, "Because none of this means anything to me anymore." After that, they sat in silence until we reached Sing-Sing. When I got back to Tappan, even some correctional officers which heard of my mother's death expressed their condolence. On the next service day, Pastor Ephraim Rivera prayed for me with other brothers in the chapel. I could feel the support of a family and God's love. Even this loss was a learning experience.

A New Day

Inmate Pastor Ephraim lived up in Sing-Sing. All the other Christian leaders which had lived in Tappan at onetime, had gone home. The Christians in Tappan were new in the Lord. They knew I was one of the Bible teachers and Ephraim's assistance. So, they looked at me for answers to their Bible questions. As

I did with David and Ephraim when I first arrived. I felt as if the Lord had advanced me in the ministry. It was a new beginning, and a new day for me. I knew I had to be an example and I worked on it.

Elliot's Loss

Some days later, I received mail from Elliot. In the letter, he told me his younger brother was stabbed to death. I quickly called his mother to find out more on what happened and why. I also wanted know how Elliot was doing. How was he taking his younger brother's death? Elliot's mother informed me that in all the pain and suffering, she had to be grateful. The night before her youngest son's death, she had invited him to church. He went with her and accepted Christ as Lord and Savior. The next day, someone her son knew, called him into a building lobby and killed him. Elliot, she explained, was holding on to the Lord for strength. Having a recent, unexpected loss myself helped me identify with Elliot's loss.

Chapter 20

PAROLE BOARD AND NIGHTMARES

MONTHS WERE PASSING AND MY TURN TO appear before the parole board was near. Soon it would be me who would get a chance at freedom. Things were different now. I felt hopeful. I was a Christian and that meant a lot to me, not that it matters to the parole board, but it did to me. I had my high school diploma; I was no longer a high school dropout; that made a great difference for me and I hoped for the board too. At least I knew the parole board could not use it against me saying, "You don't have a diploma." I was also in touch with my contact in Puerto Rico and applied to transfer my parole to Puerto Rico. Things seemed well, and I believe they would continue going well. At night, though, I was haunted by nightmares.

I constantly dreamed, as the day to my parole board hearing approached, that I was wanted by the police for a murder. In my dream, I would always find myself running from the police and knowing that they were looking for me to send me back to prison. In the dream, I would tell myself, "I should have never taken the gun in the first place, and this would have never happened." I would then wake up, realizing it was only a dream, but I would remind myself, "Never touch a gun again."

A second dream haunted me. In this dream, I was going to the parole board again, after having been home. I went back to prison, did another eight and a half years, and I had to see the board. The nightmare consists of the threat of a two-year hit at the parole board. My mental argument in the dream would be me telling myself I was going to get hit at the board for coming back. Yet, in my defense, I would comfort myself by telling me that I did so well in the streets for so long, that I knew the board would set me free. Then again, I would tell myself, "No, but you came back and that shows no matter how good you did, you will never change." I would wake up, and to my relief, it was only a dream. I would then tell myself, "I am never coming back. I am never going to make that mistake.

Pastor Ephraim Rivera had a saying that I respected very much. He would tell the Christian inmates, especially those who had come back to prison after going home, "To go home and stay home, all you have to do is want to stay home. You do not have to be a Christian to go home and stay home. All you have to do to stay home is just want your freedom more than anything." He would continue, "You need Christ, but you need Christ to be saved, not to stay home. Many of you, come back to prison, and say it's because you forgot to pray. No person is arrested for not praying. You were arrested when you committed a crime or violated parole." I agreed with what pastor Ephraim was saying, because I understood him clearly. I shouldn't hurt a person or take someone's money because I stopped going to church. That would be justifying my wrong doings.

Paroled and Released

As I listened to the news, and heard of murders, attempted murders and cop shootings or killings. Whether in New York City or any other state. I would think for a second, "The parole board is going to make an example out of me." I even heard the news of a young Black woman, found dead in the trunk of a car. The news channel informed that her parents worked as members of the parole board. It was a moment of tension. Then, I would tell myself, "No, God is in control and his will shall be done."

Finally, the month of my parole hearing came. It was March of 1993. Inmates had to dress in the green state uniform. The inmates from Tappan went together with the inmates from Sing-Sing to the parole hearing. There was a lot of pacing back and forth being done, and that included me.

I had been praying, "Lord, don't let the parole board ask me about past cases." (I had been arrested in the past for other minor stuff). I continued praying in my mind, "Lord, give me wisdom to answer whatever questions they ask me." Rumor had it that the parole board would ask trick questions or try and provoke inmates to get them upset.

Finally, my turn came, and I walked in the room. There were about four people sitting across the table facing me. There was another person on my left side and one on my right side. I even believed I saw one sitting behind me. Once I walked in, I sat in a chair in the middle of the room. I faced the people that did matter and they were the ones in front of me. A woman spoke and she was the only one who did all the speaking. "How are you, George?" I answered "I'm OK." I was so nervous, I mentioned my past cases, but the lady said, "Marrero, forget those cases; they are in the past." Then, she continued, "Marrero, you are not the same person who got arrested. You are a different person now, right?" She was very kind, as a mother advising a child. In my mind I said, "I am a new person in Christ," and I answered, "I am not the same person; I am a new person." Then, she said words that brought great joy to me. "It is up to you now not to come back to prison here or in Puerto Rico where you are being paroled to." I said, "Yes, thank you ma'am." I got up and walked out of the room. Inside of me I was dancing, jumping, and rejoicing.

When I got back to Tappan, an old-timer who called himself lord Sha-Sha, asked me, "How did it go at the board?" I told him, "I am going home." Sha-Sha quickly said, "No 'G,' man don't say that, I don't want to see you hurt." I continued, "Listen Sha-Sha—I waited a long time for this man, and ain't nobody taking this joy away. I'm going home!" Sha then said, "I respect that." I knew what Sha-Sha was trying to tell me, but I also believed I was going home so I didn't want to hear him.

That very evening we were going to receive an answer from the parole board, to know if we were going home or not. The parole response was supposed to come in with the regular mail, but that evening when the mail came, there was nothing from

155

the parole board. When we asked what happened, we were told that the results were down in the office, held there by the sergeant's orders. "Incredible, there was no reason for this," I thought to myself, and anxiety rose. Since the yard was still open, I went outside.

Once outside, I ran into an Italian American officer who was always asking me, "When are you going home?" When I saw him, I told him I went to the parole board and was waiting for the answers from the board and that the answers were in the office.

I also told him that waiting was torture. He told me "Quick, give me your full name." Once I gave it to him, he went in the office, looked quickly through the envelopes to find my name. He found my results, put it inside his shirt, walked outside and told me to follow him. I followed him; he turned, gave me the envelope and said, "Now, tell me if you are going home." I opened it quick. It was dark but I looked and saw what said, "Open Date." Open date meant I was going home. I told the officer "I am going home! I'm going home!" "Good, I'm very happy for you," he responded to me.

Later that night, when the yard was closed and all the inmates were back in the dorms, the pack of envelope were brought in and given to the officer on the floor. These were the parole results. The officer gave them out. There were quite a few and everyone was on the officer, so he did not notice that I had mine already.

Now, in the dorm, I again opened my results, this time not worrying that I would be caught with the result before time. This time, I read it calmly and clearly. The date I was scheduled to leave read June 1, which meant I could leave on that very day or any time after that date. Suddenly, fear struck me; I asked myself, "Where am I going after all these years in prison?" I shook it off and told myself, "God is in control."

From that day until the day I left to go home, I was doing a lot of thinking. "How were the streets after so many years in prison?" I was concerned that no one knew me on the outside anymore, this was not the 1980s. My prison reputation was not going to follow me. What worried me about that was that in prison once your reputation follows you, inmates know not to mess with you, especially if you are not posing a threat anymore, but in society, will people try me? If they do, will I pass the test? Will I be able to walk away or manage the situation without violence? I had to adjust to a new lifestyle in society.

When June 24, 1993 came, an excellent officer, knowing that my flight was to Puerto Rico the very next day, made sure that all my paperwork was done on time. He went beyond his responsibilities to help me. Pictures were taken when a person was arrested, pictures were taken when an inmate is released. The officer in charge of taking the pictures did not want to take my pictures because he was on break. The officer escorting me pleaded with him, telling him, "Don't do it for him, do it for me." He kept at it until the officer took the pictures.

That same night, Tappan was declared under a lockdown, inmates are not allowed to move under any circumstances in a lockdown. Yet, I was sent to Sing-Sing at the same moment the lockdown was declared. The person who was to do the last of my paperwork told me, "Someone in heaven loves you." I asked her why she said that and she explained to me, "First of all, Tappan is in lockdown. Second, I called the officer asking for another inmate, and the officer told me I called the wrong dorm, but then he told me Marrero is going up." She continued, "I was about to close the office door, to which I have no keys; you would have had to wait until Monday for this door to be opened again. Your release papers are in here. Someone in heaven loves you." I just smiled and said, "Yes." I knew I had nothing to worry about, I knew God was parting the Red Sea of obstacles.

Chapter 21

REACHING PUERTO RICO

ON JUNE 25, 1993, I WAS RELEASED AND ON my way to Puerto Rico, to start a new life. I arrived to Puerto Rico at around 3:15 p.m. I called my parole officer to the phone number I was given with my release papers. It was a Friday, and the person that answered the phone told me it was late, "Come in early Monday morning, don't worry about anything, we will see you then." I was surprised at how friendly the person sounded. "Okay, I will see you Monday then."

Early Monday morning I was present, only to learn that the parole officer did not know about my case. At least that's what she said and I wasn't about to argue with her. "You are from where, New York City? Who approved this case, let me see your folder? You have a violent crime." She continued, "Who approved this case? What part of Puerto Rico are you from?" I told her, "I never lived in Puerto Rico." "You what? You never lived in Puerto Rico? Let me tell you something, if I had taken this case, I would have never approved it." "I don't know who approved this case, but I am going to find out and I am going to start approving their cases, to see if they like it."

159

The parole officer was steaming, but hearing her say she would not have approved my case, helped me see how God had opened doors for me to be in Puerto Rico. Shortly after that encounter, my case was transferred to another parole officer and to a few others after that, until my parole was dismissed for good conduct in 1998. This was the only negative experience I had with a parole officer in Puerto Rico. I was not going to let it ruin my joy.

Puerto Rico wasn't what I expected, in some areas you could see the poverty. In other areas one could see development. The people were friendly, but they were proud. They were definitely not the 'Puerto Ricans' one is used to seeing in New York. I could see these were the real Puerto Ricans, born and raise in their land. That's where the pride came from. Many things about Puerto Rico also remind me of New York in the 1970s and 80s. Not in a bad way but in a positive way. It was as if God was giving me years back. I was amaze and remember that while I was still incarcerated, I heard preachers speak on how God can give us our time back. They would usually quote the prophet Joel 2:25 for a message like this one. I use to think to myself, "Now, that is a bit difficult to do. Once time is gone, it is gone." Yet, when I lived in the island of Puerto Rico, I thought "Even this God has done." The public phones were still a dime. The public transportation was twenty-five cents. I had so many great experiences that took me back to my teen years.

Angel Dávila

The following Sunday, after I arrived, I visited the church that I had been in contact with. I met many wonderful, humble people who welcomed me as one of their own. A Saturday after that, I went to a morning Bible study in the church. I got very involved in the class discussion. Afterwards, brother Angel Dávila who was giving the Bible study approached me. He asked me where I was studying. I told him, "I study on my own, but I plan on studying in a Bible Institute as soon as I find out where there is one." Brother Dávila said, "Listen, there is nothing wrong with a Bible Institute, but I believe you have what it takes to go to our Bible College." I told him I would think about it. I wanted to study, but I did not want to rush things. Angel did accept my answer, he was persistent, "No, you could go to the college." I told him I just came out of prison and I didn't think I was ready for college, but brother Dávila kept on insisting. He was not even listening to me say 'no.'

After that day Angel started introducing me to students from the Bible College. "Hey, this is brother George and he is going to be in the Bible College with us." I thought to myself, "Okay, he is a crazier than me." But brother Angel Dávila was not crazy, he was a man of God, an evangelist, speaking a word of faith over my life.

In the month of June, the pastor of the church was announcing that the college was about to start in August. I got happy and thought, "Maybe I can be part of the college." So, on a Sunday night after the service was over, I got up enough nerve to approach the pastor and tell him I wanted to go to the Bible College. His response to me was, "You just came home; relax, take things easy. Do not rush into things." I did not like his answer, I felt left out, but I did not want to complain. I thought, "Maybe he is right."

Instead, I became very involved in the ministry. I sat in with the Bible teachers of the church and eventually I would become one of the Bible teachers. I started preaching and evangelizing in the streets. God started to open door for me to take my testimony to the youth in different churches, schools and youth programs.

Mr. Edwin Mercado

I needed a job now, and I was introduced to one of the ministers of the church. Rev. Carmen A. Romero, who would present me to a director in an office building in Old San Juan. Mr. Edwin Mercado interviewed me for a job. One of his questions to me was, if I was ever arrested in New York City. I told him yes, to his surprise. He asked 'what for' and I answered, "An attempted murder of a police officer while in an arm robbery." He was shocked; he looked at me with wide eyes. He paused; there was silence in the room. Then, he asked how much prison time I did. I answered him, "I was sentenced to eight years and four months to twenty-five years, of which I did eight and a half years in prison."

Mr. Mercado said, "Wow, now I am sorry I asked you." This time to my surprise, he told me, "Your sincerity moves me, so I am going to give you the job anyway." I would work there for the next four years before moving on to greater blessings. Mr. Mercado proved to be very fair and just in his treatment with me. He showed me so much trust that anytime there was a job that involved currency he would call me to take care of it. After about two years, Mr. Mercado approached me and said, "George, I want to thank you, because I took a chance on you and you did well. You didn't fail me." I thanked him too, for the chance he gave me.

Danny

One early morning as I was walking to my building, I notice a young man walking my way. As he got closer, I recognized him, it was my brother Danny. I called him, he looked puzzled. At first, he did not recognize me. It had been years since we saw each other. Even when he knew it was me, he said "I can't talk right now." He seemed shy and confuse, I remembered I was told he was struggling with addition. Although, we did not speak then I would see him many times afterward. Because I was ministering in the streets, I met a lot of people from the streets. Because they learned Danny was my brother, they would always tell me where he was. Many times, I took him to programs and a few other times I let him spend the night and fed him. As a Christian this was my responsibility. We would have long conversations at times. I could see how smart he was. I told him I never understood why he dropped out of high school having only one semester to go. We remembered our youth and laughed a lot about many things. We spoke about mom and how things could have been better. He would defender her and say she did the best she could, I would laugh and tell him, "Yeah, you were her favorite." I then asked him if he seen his daughters, he said not recently. So, I took him to see them. Before I left Puerto Rico to return to the U.S. mainland Danny was studying short courses, attending church and in touch with his daughters.

Chapter 22

STARTING BIBLE COLLEGE

A YEAR LATER, THE PASTOR OF THE CHURCH was promoted to overseer of the Mission Board churches of Puerto Rico. A new pastor was installed to our local church — Reverend Pedro Cintrón, an attorney by profession. Rev. Cintrón was very happy and willing to help out in his new position of service to the church. I approached Rev. Cintrón and spoke to him about my interest of studying at the Bible College. Immediately, Rev. Cintrón told me, "Bring me the documents that I have to sign as your pastor and I will sign them." Rev. Cintrón knew I was actively teaching in the church and preaching in the streets and in other churches when invited.

By now, going to the Bible College wasn't something brother Dávila had to push me into doing. It was something I desired with a passion. I had lost the fear of going to college; the year I was told to wait, I used to find out all I could about the Bible College. When the time came, I went to the college to do the paperwork and the arrangements to enroll. I arrived at the *Colegio Biblico Pentecostal* of the Mission Board Council in Saint Just, Puerto

Rico. (On present time the university is known as: *Universidad Teológica del Caribe*).

As part of the process of being accepted, I had to take a test consisting of at least one hundred questions on the Bible, to evaluate my biblical knowledge. I took it and did very well. I was then interviewed by the staff. The lady interviewing me, asked me if I thought I could make it through the four years to obtain my degree. She then asked me what motivated me to enroll? I told her, "I like studying the Bible and I really want to learn more. Plus, there is an Evangelist named Nicky Cruz. I think he was crazier than I was. He preaches; I heard him on a tape when I was in prison. Therefore, I think I have a shot." She laughed and told me "Yes, you have a great role model there." After everything was done, I was accepted and I was extremely happy.

My first night of class came. I walked in the classroom; I was one of the first ones there. I sat down, leaning back in my chair. I still had some street and prison swag in me. People could see it in the way I walked, sat, and spoke. I was not your regular college student that was for sure. As I sat in the class, other students started coming in. Some came in with their briefcases, others with their suits and ties. They were very well dressed, looking very professional. Many were pastors and chaplains; some of them had a degree already and were doing a second degree. Suddenly, some fear struck, and I asked myself, "What are you doing in here? This isn't for you. You are in a real college. You just wanted to study the Bible in an institute, something basic. This is for professionals, not you." But as the class started, I got a hold of myself and relaxed and told myself, "Let's try it." The experience turned out to be a very good one and the beginning of my academic life style.

In the first semester, I only took two classes to feel things out. It was not easy; another problem I had was the language. Being born and raised in New York, my primary language was English. I learned my Spanish was not as good as I thought. It seemed like everyone who met me would ask me, "You are from the United States, right?" I would answer, "Yeah, how did you know?" After a while, I realized it had to do with the way I spoke Spanish. My accent gave me away. Yet, I was determined, I was not going to give up. "I will just work on my Spanish, until I can read it, write it, and speak it well enough," and that is what I did.

Beside from the difficulty in the language, the experience in the theological university was one of learning, growth, and meeting wonderful people—that included each and every one of my professors. I was humbled by the experience, each of my professors played an important role in my Christian growth, academic learning, and even in my emotional aspect. Every time I took a course that had to do with human development, psychology, counseling or family relationship, I would take it as a student, but also acknowledging that the class could also be a healing process.

I then met a sister in one of my classes, who introduced me to a group of chaplains and the Lord opened doors for me to enter one of the biggest prisons in Puerto Rico known as *El Oso*

Blanco, where I was able to go and share my testimony and preach the word of God.

A year after starting college, my daughter Deborah was born, a blessing from God. For the next four years I would take her to class every night with me until I graduated, obtaining a bachelor's degree in Arts with a major in Christian Education. My daughter marched with me in my graduation. She too wore a cap and gown herself. This was amazing. God had blessed me beyond what I ever could imagined, I remembered there was a time when I thought because of the time I was facing in prison that I would never have children. Yet, here I was graduating and with my little girl by my side. My father also came to my graduation and spent time with us. God was doing wonderful things in my life.

Completely Free

One morning, I went to report to the parole office and I took my daughter with me. When I entered the building, I was received by Miss Otero, who had been my parole officer at one time. She seemed so happy for me. I did not understand what her joy was. Then, she told me, "Congratulations, you are finally free." I said, "It is 1998, I've been out for five years now." She continued "No, I mean from your parole; your release papers came in from Albany, New York, releasing you! You are no longer on parole!" After five years out on parole I was finally free, completely free! I was so overwhelmed with joy; it felt better than when I was released from prison itself.

Being released from parole and eventually graduating were great experiences for me, but it couldn't stop there. So, I enrolled in the Evangelical Seminary of Puerto Rico, to do a Masters in Religion. I was even given a scholarship and did not have to pay for my studies. By now, I was confident and looking forward to my studies. I was not worried. I had grown, and healed in many areas.

I then applied to teach and was hired by the Wesleyan Academy of Guaynabo Puerto Rico. There, I taught for three years growing in new experiences. I was even blessed with enrolling my daughter in the academy, where she received a Christian education and an excellent academic education in a wonderful environment. The experience of teaching in Wesleyan Academy was amazing. I taught students who were the sons and daughters of judges, politicians, lawyers, and law enforcement. Who would tell me I would be doing these things when I was incarcerated? I would praise God silently in my heart as I taught the class.

[Speedy, Peanut, Gee early 1980s]

[Speedy, Ed, Gee, Big George]

[B.A. Graduation, Bible College with daughter Débora]

[M.A. Graduation, S.E.P.R. Maria, Prof. Perez, dgt. Débora, George]

[Elliot and George in Puerto Rico]

[George, wife Maria and kids in D.C.]

[Gee, Life, Peanut, in Harlem N.Y.]

[Speedy, Peanut, George 2020]

Chapter 23

HARDSHIP AND GRACE

PROFESSOR DR. DAVID FRANKLYN IN A CLASS
I took, spoke these words. "God hates divorce, because God loves families. But if you go through a divorced tomorrow, remember in all things God works for the good of those who love him." I felt God was speaking to me.

By the year 2001, a crisis would strike, and I would go through a divorce. In this difficult moment, I was fortunate to have brothers and sisters in the Lord who gave me words of encouragement, and sound advice. I thank God for them. In time, many told me how much they admired the fact that I continued my studies and went forward in life. Some told me they knew people that turned to their old ways because of crisis such as divorce. To those I answered, "When I accepted Christ in my life, I did it willingly and with a sound mind. I don't see why I should stop serving Christ because of challenges we face in life."

On an occasion when Big George visit Puerto Rico he shared with me about his divorce experience. He told me when his father found out about his divorce, his father stood quiet for a minute. Then his father just said, "**Life goes on**." Those words became so real to me in that moment. Having had some people which did not know what happened, but they were quick to judge. As seemed to be the case in many occasions.

On another occasion visiting the Bible College in which I had studied. I saw and spoke with Professor, Dr. Fausto Lora. I shared with Dr. Lora I had pass through a divorce. Dr. Lora said, "George I have to be honest with you I have a class that starts right now, but I have to tell you, **Life goes on.**" I don't know if George and Dr. Lora knew how powerful and uplifting these short words were to me. But they were very effective.

I accepted life would go on after a divorce. In my life I have been through tougher situation, but what about ministering? I had been so active in ministry in so many ways. Then on two separate occasions, while listening to WBMJ 1190 AM, a Christian radio station, I heard a pastor speaking. He went on to say, "We give our pulpits to ex-murderers, because we say God is a God of forgiveness and love, and that he is. But when we know of a person who went through a divorce, we act as if God cannot forgive them." He continued preaching, "Listen to me you who have gone through a divorce; God's plans will be fulfilled in your life. A divorce is not the end of your ministry or God's purpose for your life."

On a second occasion, I remember hearing a group of divorced men and women speaking on how the Lord was helping them organize their life again after a divorce. They were speaking about giving themselves a second chance in marriage. Starting a new relationship was part of God's healing process in their lives. It was not by coincidence that I heard these messages on the radio; God was speaking to me. I praised God because never before had I heard such a clear message on God's forgiveness for people that have been through a divorce.

Chapter 24

THE EVANGELICAL SEMINAR OF PUERTO RICO

THE EVANGELICAL SEMINARY OF PUERTO Rico was founded in 1919. Dr. Martin Luther King, Jr. had preached there in the past. This is a historical seminary I was in. The professors were beyond excellent; they all had PhDs and seemed to have the correct answers to any of the student question or comments. All a student had to do was bring up a topic and the professors would know what book, author, or theologian they were speaking about, I was amazed. Even the seminar's geographical location was great. Located on the Ponce De Leon Avenue, across the street from the University of Puerto Rico, in the metropolitan area. I was thrilled to be here.

Like in the theological university, I was present in every special event. Sitting in to hear theologians, historians, and anthropologists speak. These were special events that took place besides the regular courses taken in a semester. It was impressing to see scholars and experts in the field that was touched upon. It wasn't just someone who knew about history, but a historian. It wasn't

Maria T. Rosario

On this one specific semester, while taking a course on Human Sexuality, with professor and sexologist Dr. Gloria Mock. Every time I went into the class, there was only one chair available. The chair was always next to the same student. Her name, I would learn, was Maria Teresa. She was a familiar face; I had seen her in some of my other classes. But we never spoke. Now I would come in and sit quietly next to her. I would then ask Maria in a whispering tone, "Update me on the topic." Maria would put me up to date on the topic. Though she wasn't too amused with the fact that she could observe that I was a New Yorker by the way I spoke Spanish. She also thought to herself, "He is a little crazy, like a New Yorker." At least this was her perception of me at the moment.

Maria's political view were those of the Puerto Rican Independent Party. She had promised herself as a teen that she would not even date a Nuyorican, as some Puerto Ricans call us New Yorkers of Puerto Rican descent. Even less marry one, but we became friends.

Maria was a youth pastor and an elementary school teacher. She was the oldest of three siblings. She graduated with a bachelor's degree in education from the University of Puerto Rico. She was now working on her master's degree in Divinity. She appeared to me like a very smart and interesting person, but after going through a divorce, even though approximately three years had passed I was not interested in meeting someone. Plus, she seemed too nice and honest, and that puzzled me a bit. "Where do people like this come from?" I would think. "Are they real?"

I started to realize that although I was involved in the ministry, I was ministering to people with a similar past to what I had at one time in my life. I didn't totally get away from a life style I once lived. I was still preaching to inmates; I would preach in the *caserios*—housing projects in Puerto Rico equal to New York City housing projects. Many of the *caserios* in Puerto Rico are for low-income families, where poverty and crime are high. This observation was a learning experience.

Maybe that's why Maria seemed like such a nice person to me. I observed her and wondered if we could date. But up to now I never tried even asking her out on a date. Then the semester was over. The Christmas break came, and we would not return until January 2004. Once the new semester began, I was in the library at the seminar. I looked across the room and the first person I saw coming my way was Maria. Her curly black hair was shining. I could see in her face that she had lost some weight. I was speechless. I went over to her and said "Hi," and she said hi, but because I saw she was studying, I left.

I would see Maria again in a chapel service we had, where all classes were required to attend. She sat a few rows in front of me and I told myself, "I can't be afraid of starting a new relationship. It's now or never." Once the service was over, I asked her for her cellular number and she gave it to me. A few days later, I called her and she was busy. I called again another day and she was busy. Every time I called, she seemed busy. I remember once she told me she was correcting her student's grades. I told myself, "I corrected my student grades too, and I finished." So, I did not call back and I plan on not calling back anymore. Until about a month pass and I thought, "She is a nice young lady, maybe she really was busy." So, I called and asked her if she was up for a movie. She said yes and we had our first date. As time went on, our friendship grew. We were always very respectful to each other and understanding. We had great communication with each other and trust.

After some time, when I saw we were doing well in our friendship, I presented my daughter to her. I spoke to my daughter about María and let her know we were just friends and we were getting to know each other. To God, I prayed a simple prayer, "Lord, let your will be done." My daughter and María got along very well and they became friends.

In time, I graduated, obtaining my master's degree. María and my daughter both attended my graduation, sharing with me in this new victory the Lord had made possible. After the ceremony was over, I took my daughter back to her mother. María and I continued sharing. We had a beautiful evening and I drove her back to the seminary where she was living. We sat on the benches in the garden of the seminary. There, we spoke about our friendship and I asked her what she wanted out of it, what were her plans, and we told each other how we felt about each other. We then made our courtship official and on June 11, of 2005, we got married. Since then, God has blessed us with two more family members, our son George D. and our youngest daughter, Genesis. God has been great, a faithful and mighty God that guides our lives.

Chapter 25

CONCLUSION

Life Is an Ongoing Responsibility, Never Look Back

MY WIFE WENT ON TO GRADUATE, OBTAINING her Master's in Divinity, this time I was the one attending her graduation. I then started my PhD in History of the Americas in the Interamerican University of Cupey, Puerto Rico. I would also be called by various universities in Puerto Rico, to teach on their campuses. I would teach until I returned to the United States, leaving the island where my parents were born, the island my parents left in the late 1950s to come to the US.

The beautiful island of Puerto Rico had opened its tropical heart to me—the island with so many loving, wonderful people. After living in Puerto Rico for twenty-three years, I to became a Puerto Rican even if it was by adoption. I learned its history, asking like a little kid what each political symbol meant the first time I saw them when I first stepped foot on the island. I learned the ideology of each party and what they represented. Yet now

I was leaving, but not with empty hands as when I first arrived. Now I was leaving as a husband, a father, and a professional.

On this return trip, my oldest daughter Deborah, was flying with me, she had just obtained her bachelor's degree. I was so proud and excited of her. My wife and two younger children would arrive to New York six month later. I returned to the United States trusting God goes before me and my family. May his will continue to lead our lives.

My purpose for telling my story is not to praise violence or a thug life style. There are events of my past life I intentionally left out. I do not see it necessary to share every violent act or every detail of events. I shared enough to speak about true change. I am telling my story, because I want to tell the world that God is real and his power to transform lives is real. For God so loves you that he gave his son Jesus Christ to die in your place. As, he rose Jesus from the dead, he can rise you into a new life. I hope this story is of inspiration to you.

GLOSSARY

Bodega: Store.

Dios mio, Dios mio: My God, My God.

El hijo del diablo: The son of the devil.

El vecindario es de morenos: It's a black/African American neighborhood.

En casa no lo quiero: I don't want him in my house.

fuego, fuego, salgan, avanza: fire, fire, get out, hurry.

Hay Dios mío, ya mismo este viene borracho a pelear: Oh my God, soon he is coming drunk to fight.

Los Ciento Veinte: The One hundred Twenty

No le hablo más: I will not speak to him anymore.

Papi: Daddy

papi, yo te conozco: daddy, I know you.

Perdon mi amor: forgive me my love.

Si, tranquilo: Okay, relax.

Sentí la presencia de Dios mientras hablabas. I felt God's presence as you spoke.

Teatro Puerto Rico: Puerto Rico Theater

Y los nenes, busca los nenes: and the kids, look for the kids.